Moms Make a Difference

LINDSEY O'CONNOR

HARVEST HOUSE PUBLISHERS
Eugene, Oregon 97402

Cover by Paz Design Group, Salem, Oregon

MOMS MAKE A DIFFERENCE
Copyright © 1999 by Lindsey O'Connor
Published by Harvest House Publishers
Eugene, Oregon 97402

Library of Congress Cataloging-in-Publication Data

O'Connor, Lindsey, 1961–
    Moms make a difference / Lindsey O'Connor.
        p. cm.
    Originally published: Moms who changed the world. Eugene, Or.: Harvest House, 1999.
    ISBN 0-7369-0616-9
        1. Mothers. 2. Motherhood. 3. Mothers—Religious life. I. Title.
[HQ759.O32342   2001]
306.874'3—dc21   00-047124

Printed in the United States of America

01 02 03 04 05 06 / BP-PH / 10 9 8 7 6 5 4 3 2 1

To Tim—
Your agape in action enabled these words.

Contents

My Thanks and Appreciation to ...

Tim, my partner in life and ministry. Thank you for encouraging me to write this book, then making it possible to do so (you are an amazing man and father!). Thank you for leading me with the tandem blessing of godly wisdom and a sense of humor.

Jacquelyn, Claire, Collin, and Allison for being such fabulous children. Thanks for all your prayers, coffee service, and nachos while I wrote. Claire—incredible job, my dear! I couldn't have done this without you.

Susan Gragg, my kindred spirit, whose deep insight and unwavering support helped shape this project. You sharpen my thinking and make me a better writer. Only you know just when to say, "Lindsey, that's the worst sentence you've ever written" and when to get out your pom-poms!

Kathy Groom for laughing at the right spots, encouraging me in the rough spots, and reminding me to get to know Amy. Thanks to you and Tom for the retreat at Groom Acres.

The Frey family for allowing and helping me to tell your mother's and grandmother's story.

Those who prayed for me and this book, especially my Dad and Barbara. Also Donna Patchell, Cheri Fuller, Char Barnes, Lois Deyo, Linda Vias, and Becky Simms. (Linda and Becky, you helped me so much.)

Becky Freeman, my gifted friend, whose creative suggestions revived me better than a double, tall cappuccino when book A became book B. You'll see your influence in these pages. And Linda Shepherd, for the hospitality and solitude of Shepherd's Rest.

James Manship of Statesman Communications for your invaluable expertise and suggestions that helped reflect a more accurate Mary Washington.

Kathy Currie, the Mary Ball Washington Museum curator, and Carla Wing, the Mary Washington House hostess for your insights into this interesting lady and her times.

The Littleton Historical Museum staff, the Castle Rock Library staff, and the Denver Seminary Library staff for research assistance and help in locating some rare books.

Peter Van Luen at Readex for permission to quote from *The American Women's Diaries Collection*, and Zena Robinson for your assistance in combing through that material.

My Harvest House friends: Terry Glaspey, Carolyn McCready, and LaRae Weikert for your enthusiasm and ideas. Terry, for your skillful editing and your encouragement to be creative when I told you I wanted to try something a little different with the "Just Imagine" sections. You challenge me to pursue excellence.

A Note from
the Author

─────◦

*T*he old expression "the hand that rocks the cradle rules the world" may be a bit overstated (what mom feels like a world ruler during a 2:00 A.M. night feeding?), so perhaps we should say this: The hand that rocks the cradle can *change* the world. Like the moms in this book did.

This book is *not* a top-ten list of the greatest moms in the world (where would one even begin?). It's not an exhaustive study of these women's lives (go to a full-length biography for that). It's not an academic dissertation (I'm a mother with a journalism background, *not* a historian).

Instead, what I've tried to do is to take a look at a few people who've made a difference in the world and the imprint their mothers left on their lives. Think of it as a collection of snapshots; it's not a movie of their lives, but some isolated moments that give you a glimpse of who they were and how they impacted their children and the world, or at least their corner of it.

I'm not overlooking the immeasurable importance of fathers. Nor do I deny the significance of other factors: the people and experiences that make up our lives or our own innate character. All these things are important. Without devaluing any of them, I want to highlight the crucial weight of a mother's influence.

There are so many qualities in each of these mothers that I could have discussed, but instead I decided to focus upon one outstanding trait that I saw in each of them. They were not perfect moms (that's only in the movies), just like we are not, so we can easily relate to these women and learn from them.

I wrote this book much the same way I would talk to you about these moms if we were having a cup of tea or coffee together. I try to provide a window into their lives, their character, and how they impacted me (because each one did). I also included a "Just Imagine…" section in each chapter, where I speculated on what it might have been like to meet them. As I began to learn about these women, I started to feel like I knew them. So, I had a little fun and pretended I could travel back to their time. While fiction, these scenes contain much fact. They are based upon events that really happened, snippets of their letters, or quotes about them. There is also a box at the beginning of each chapter that highlights the achievements of their famous offspring. Reading the "Look Who Rocked the World" first may help you better understand some things you read about the mom later in the chapter.

These moms have impacted me. By getting to know them I have been convicted, comforted, challenged, and encouraged. Their stories have made me want to be a better mom. I pray they do the same for you.

—*Lindsey O'Connor*

ONE

Susanna Wesley

The Mother of John and Charles Wesley

1669 – 1742

Look Who Rocked the World

WHO: *John and Charles Wesley*

WHAT: *Cofounders of Methodism. Leaders of the Evangelical revival in the Church of England in the eighteenth century. John was a renowned evangelist and theologian, preaching over 42,000 sermons and writing 233 books. Charles was a prolific hymn writer, with over 8000 hymns to his credit.*

WHEN: *John, 1703–1791, Charles, 1707–1788*

WHERE: *England*

After being schooled by their mother, John and Charles left home for boarding school—John to Charterhouse and Charles to Westminster. Later they both attended and received degrees from Christ Church, Oxford. It was there at Oxford that the seeds of Methodism began to grow when Charles formed a society called the Holy Club—a group of men who met regularly for methodical study and prayer. It is here, in 1729, that Charles and John first earned the title "Methodist," but more importantly, it is this group that served as the nucleus for the beginning of revival.

But even though John and Charles received their degrees, became ordained priests in the Anglican Church, and even endured a treacherous missionary journey to America, neither really knew Christ as his personal Savior. Believing that salvation comes by good works, the Wesley boys, fearful about their standing before God, were determined to earn their place in heaven. As John wrote after his failed missionary journey: "I went to convert others, who will convert me? Who, what is he that will deliver me from this evil heart of unbelief? I have a fair summer religion. I can talk well; nay, and believe myself, while no danger is near. But let death look me in the face, and my spirit is troubled."[1]

But try as he might, and work as he did, that assurance of salvation he searched for wasn't to be his until many years later when, at a meeting in Aldersgate Street, he felt his heart "strangely warmed" and understood that salvation came by grace alone. Charles had come to the same realization only months prior. Their experience led to a sweeping revival.

The preaching of truth, the writing of marvelous hymns, the formation of a whole new church structure, the founding of hospitals for the sick, homes for orphans, schools for the poor, active opposition to slavery, and traveling over a quarter of a million miles to spread the gospel of Jesus Christ—these are the ways in which John and Charles Wesley rocked the world.

And it all began at their mother's knee.

Susanna Wesley

A Mom of Disciplined Faithfulness

———•••———

"I learned more about Christianity from my mother than
from all the theologians of England."

—JOHN WESLEY

———•••———

*T*he goal for the day," I said enthusiastically,
"is to find out what died in the pantry.
Who's game?"

"Eeeeewwww!" replied the two younger children as they
wrinkled their noses.

"I'm sure I have lots of homework, but thanks for the offer,
Mom," Claire said. "I'll bet Jacquelyn would love to do it."

"Do what?" she said brightly as she entered the kitchen.

"Find the dead thing in the pantry," Collin eagerly volunteered.

"Oh yuck! Like a mouse?"

"No, like a vegetable," I replied.

"That's still gross."

"Well, you look like just the person for the job," I said, then
I noticed that Allison was wearing one red sock, one purple
sock, and a nightgown from the dress-up box. "Alli, you're sup-
posed to be ready to leave. Please change. We leave in…oh my,
four minutes."

"Actually, Mom," Jacquelyn interjected, "I was wondering if you have any matching socks that I can borrow and...do you think I could go to that Christian concert Friday night?"

"Well...how good are you at finding dead things?"

"You're serious aren't you?"

"Go for it, Sherlock." I looked at my watch and realized I had twenty minutes of things to do in the remaining three minutes. I began to fly around the house giving staccato directions. I felt like a cross between Road Runner and Old Mother Hubbard.

"Mom?"

"Yes?"

"What are we doing tomorrow?"

"I'll tell you as soon as I figure out what we're doing today... oh, I know. We're going back to the Not-to-Be-Ignored-Family-Schedule-and-Chore-Chart posted on the bulletin board. Now, let's scoot!"

Later that afternoon, with appointments kept, errands run, and children deposited in various locations, I stood in my friend's warm, sunny kitchen for a rare moment of childfree woman-talk. I sat on the counter and looked out Kathy's window at the field and the distant mountains, which had been dusted with a fresh coat of powdered-sugar snow—the first of the year. I sipped my hot tea as she took a tray of homemade cookies out of the oven. The aroma of chocolate and vanilla filled the air.

"Well, I definitely had a Gomer Pyle morning," I said. "I think my natural bent on the structure scale falls somewhere between General Schwartzkopf and Lucy Ricardo. What about you?" I asked.

"It depends. Which day are we talking about?" she said with a big grin. Her silver-and-green earrings perfectly matched her chartreuse sweater. She looked more like a cookie-baking model than June Cleaver. "But you're a lot more disciplined than I am," she said.

"Only when I work hard at it. We're moms in process, aren't we?"

"Definitely," she laughed. "I love the results of having a structured routine, even though it's not how I'm hard-wired. It makes family life go so much smoother. I guess what I want is structure with flexibility."

"Ooh, the great paradox!"

We dissolved into laughter as we reached for a hot cookie, knowing that our more naturally structured friends wouldn't find that nearly as funny as we did.

Kathy faced me and her eyes sparkled.

"You know, I've learned that I *can* be taught, though. I owe so much to the example of my sister-in-law, Rita. I'm trying to be the transitional generation in my family, and she truly inspires me."

I left Kathy's that day warmed by good friendship and conversation (not to mention good cookies) and thought of the importance of inspiring examples. Susanna Wesley has become one for me. In getting to know Susanna, I discovered a woman not only of rigid order and routine, but also of disciplined *faithfulness*. She inspires me! I would love to talk with her. If only I could...perhaps as a neighbor attending the Sunday evening services she led in her home.

Just Imagine . . .

The Rectory, Epworth, London,
The Home of Samuel and Susanna Wesley, 1712

Yellow light spilled invitingly from the thirteen windows of the red-brick house and curls of smoke rose upward from the three chimneys. I couldn't wait to arrive. A small group of people behind me were also walking toward the Rectory, but I arrived first and knocked on the door. It opened cautiously and a maid peeked her capped head through the crack.

"Good evenin' to you and come in, but you be the last one," she said, letting me squeeze through. I stepped into the center hall and heard the maid greet the group who had been behind me. "Nay, tisn't any more room. Try again next week."

The frigid wind blew a sprinkling of snow into the house as she shut the door. "That's all this house'll hold," she announced. "There's nigh to 200 folks here tonight."

I turned from her to the crowd in the hall that was overflowing from the kitchen and strained my ears to hear the voice that was addressing them. I could just barely make out her exhortations on honoring the Lord's day, then she began to read from Scripture. I listened intently, as did everyone else in the house, including the children. Time passed quickly and before I realized it, Mrs. Wesley was concluding in prayer.

I moved to the corner of the hall as people began to file past me on their way out. I had to speak privately to this woman. She was surrounded by people asking her questions, so I spotted a stool in the corner and sat down to wait for the crowd to disperse.

The furnishings in the home were practical and far from numerous. From where I sat there appeared to be no clutter anywhere. The nursemaid went by holding a child by each hand, as they silently followed her up the stairs to get ready for bed. As the last of the evening visitors departed, all I could hear was the cow outside and a few soft voices. You'd never know that nine of Susanna's children were in the house. Finally seeing my opportunity, I approached her.

"Mrs. Wesley, I so enjoyed your meeting tonight. I wondered if I might have a word with you, forgiving the lateness of the hour and all." Her fair complexion and chestnut-colored hair were still beautiful at forty-three years of age. She had a serious demeanor, but looked at me with kindness in her almond-shaped eyes.

"Well, of course, my dear neighbor. So good of you to come to hear the Lord's words on this Sabbath. What is it?"

"First, I want to tell you that I think it's a grand thing that you are allowing so many to join you in these devotions you are having with your children."

She smiled. "Though I am not a man, nor a minister, and it has certainly happened by accident, I am indeed pleased that so many have begun to show an interest in God's truths," she said.

"Mrs. Wesley, I know that many in this village have given you and your family great difficulty in the past, questioning the Rector's politics and not taking very kindly to his sterner sermons and admonitions. I know someone set your house on fire and burned your field of flax. I've heard them taunting your children and making all kinds of disruptive noise outside your house at night."

"Oh, that is all true, but look at what God is doing here," she said with a twinkle in her eye.

"Bringing peace as I see it."

"As I see it as well," she said with a smile.

"I do have questions on some things you spoke of tonight, but I was wondering if I might instead ask you a question on a more personal note?"

"Certainly." She drew up a wooden chair and motioned for me to do the same.

"Everyone here in Epworth knows that the Reverend Wesley has a large brood, and that you, Madam, are a fine mother as well as a busy one. You see, my own dear mother is with our Lord now, and I have some questions on the raising of my four children. I wonder how you manage so well with your nine?"

"Ten actually. Sammy, my firstborn, is away at school," she corrected. "And that doesn't count the nine who are now in the grave, bless their souls."

"Oh, my," I stammered, trying to imagine bearing more than a dozen and a half children. "Your children behave so differently than most of the ill-mannered village children. I know that you spend a great deal of time training them, and I want to inquire as to some of your methods."

"I do follow certain methods, but I am afraid you may find them disagreeable."

"But your children seem so happy and polite and intelligent." I glanced at her immaculate kitchen, then into her eyes. "I must know how you do it."

"Very well, my dear." She shifted in her chair and smoothed her apron. "But first let's talk a bit. You're not from Epworth, are you?"

"No, London."

"Ah, we are both city girls."

"But you have cows, and chickens, and a garden," I said, surprised.

"It is amazing what one can do when one tries," she answered with a slight smile. "And when we must."

"Isn't it, though." Her strict reputation had preceded her, and I had not expected such a pleasant, gracious woman. I leaned forward in my chair. "The fire you had two years ago...was it terrible?" I asked.

"Oh...it was a dreadful night! We first discovered the fire because the roof fell in on poor Hetty's bed after we were all tucked in that night. She screamed for her father, and he yelled to us all to run for our lives as the roof was falling. It happened so quickly that we almost didn't make it down the stairs."

"How did you get the children out?"

"I screamed for Betty, our maidservant, to get the children out of the nursery. She grabbed Patty and had Jacky follow her. I tried three times to break through the flames near the street door, but they were too intense. I finally had to just wade through the fire!"

"Oh!" I instinctively rubbed my arm, imagining the scorching heat.

"But the worst part..."

"What?" I said.

"When I got to the yard, I couldn't see anyone. I thought they were all lost. Thank God, I was mistaken. But we did realize that Jacky (her nickname for John), who was five then, was missing. Samuel ran back into the burning house to try to save him and heard a miserable, heart-wrenching cry from the nursery. He tried several times to reach him, bless his heart, but he couldn't. The poor man came out in tears and commended his soul to God."

"Oh, how awful."

"But God had a plan," she said with a big grin. "Jacky had climbed up to the window and cried out. Two men in the yard got up to the casement and pulled my child out just as the roof fell into the chamber! Samuel said that sweet Jacky was 'a brand plucked from the burning!' By God's great mercy we all escaped, and I have been particularly careful of the soul of that child ever since."

"Perhaps his narrow escape signals something special."

She gave me a knowing smile and nodded in agreement.

"Mrs. Wesley?" I asked, suddenly realizing the lateness of the hour.

"Yes, dear,"

"How do you do all that you do?"

"It's very simple," she said. She suddenly rose from her chair and returned it to its place at the table. She put her arm on mine and looked me squarely in the eye. "Not easy, but simple. I focus all of my efforts into my children because I am compelled by a powerful hope. Come back next week and I shall explain." And with that she led me to the door and sweetly bid me good night.

Look Who Rocked John and Charles' Cradle

Susanna Wesley was born in 1669 in London, England, the twenty-fifth and last child of Reverend Samuel Annesley. Yes, you read that correctly—twenty-fifth! Sort of takes your breath away to think about, doesn't it? We don't know very much about all those siblings and her mother (except that she had to be *very* patient!), but we do know they provided a legacy of faith for Susanna and her famous sons. Her grandparents on her father's side were devout Puritans who raised their son to know the Lord at an early age. Arnold Dallimore wrote that at the age of five, young Annesley (Susanna's father) "began to read twenty chapters of the Bible a day and this practice he continued till the close of his life."[2] The twin emphases of intellect and piety were a family legacy. Annesley was a prominent minister and became a leading British dissenter from the Church of England.

Yet his youngest daughter did not share those views. Before she was thirteen she showed her characteristic strong independence, keen mind, and decision-making ability. She left her father's noncomformist beliefs and church to become an Anglican—the very religion he was resisting. Can you imagine the tension at dinner the night she announced *that* decision? She even wrote a paper describing her reasons for siding with the Church of England, which showed uncommon intelligence and insight for someone so young. Growing up, she read widely from her father's library and benefited from her exposure to prominent thinkers of the day. She came to know theology as well as, or better than, many clergymen.

About the time she made her church decision, she met Samuel Wesley. His parents had been dissenters as well. His father, banned from the state church for his beliefs, died in jail after refusing to stop preaching. Yet Samuel, like Susanna, chose to leave the religion of his family and embrace the Church of England, which put a greater emphasis on works, rather than preaching faith alone.

At nineteen, Susanna and Samuel married and they started a family. Over the next nineteen years they averaged one child per year. That means nineteen children, though not all survived. (Are you wondering, like I did, just how many years of pregnancy that is? Or other important questions such as, "Did she have a flat stomach?")

What strikes me about Susanna is that she was a mom who was both disciplined *and* faithful. As you read about her discipline, you may think of her like my friend who said, "Oh, she trips me up with her legalistic, rigid perfectionism. I could never be like her!" But behind Susanna's exterior I glimpse her heart...and she inspires me. Let's look together at how these two qualities can be seen in her life.

Susanna Was Disciplined

Disciplined Routine: Susanna was a mother who believed in, and practiced, a disciplined routine. She carefully structured her day, and her actions. She wrote, "The children were always put into a regular method of living, in such things as they were capable of, from their birth; as in dressing and undressing, changing their linen, etc..."[3] That reminds me of the advice I received so often as a new mom: children thrive on routine. But routine can be hard for moms like me, who lack that "structure" gene. I used to wish I could install a "routine-ometer" in my brain. Instead, I learned to balance my creative "let's have fun" side with trying to be structured once I saw the value of routine in my children's lives. Susanna had set times for everything: rising, school, meals, family prayers, bed. Every minute of every day was planned in the Wesley family. As Sandy Dengler writes in *Susanna Wesley: Servant of God,* "They began bedtime preparations at five, ate at six, held devotions privately at seven, and were tucked away by eight."[4] But a key phrase in the above quote from Susanna—"in such things as they were capable of"—shows her to be a sensitive mother who was aware of her children's limitations. She was not a cold, dictatorial mother as she is sometimes depicted.

Few people really like the feeling of being ruled by a schedule, but I think Susanna probably had to: Ten children plus no structure would have equaled chaos. She needed the routine to function. And she didn't do it all by herself. In fact, she always had a servant or two. This was a necessity for her, as she was frequently sick (with so many pregnancies), and besides, having servants was common in her day. All but the very poorest had a domestic helper.

Disciplined Child Training: Susanna is well-known for excelling at training and educating her children. She set apart a room in their home for schooling and taught them from nine to twelve, then again from two until five. Six hours of school a day, six days a week. Learning this I just wanted to say, "Ah, Susanna, give 'em a break and take 'em all to the zoo!"

They started each day with psalms and prayers, were assigned a chapter from both the Old and New Testaments, and ended with singing the psalms. They learned to read by age five (from Scripture), were well-schooled in the basics (as well as Latin), learned how to write poetry and music, and studied Greek and Hebrew in the evenings with their father. She kept them on task too. "There was no such thing as loud talking or playing allowed," stated Susanna, "but everyone was kept close to business for the six hours of school."[5] Her three sons later went off to boarding school and eventually Oxford; Sammy left first at fourteen, then John at eleven, and Charles around nine.

On one occasion Mrs. Wesley went over and over again with John a portion of a lesson that seemed impossible for him to understand. The father, sitting nearby, became irritated at the apparent stupidity of the child, and exclaimed, "Susanna, why do you tell that lad the same thing for the hundredth time?" "Because," was the calm reply, "the ninety-ninth time he did not understand."

Besides teaching them academic subjects, she established and enforced strict rules in order to train them to be obedient and well-mannered. They weren't allowed to talk at the table or idly with servants, they learned to handle a knife and fork properly, they weren't allowed to play with the rough children in Epworth, and she required respectful speech and a precise use of language.

She once wrote that she taught them from a year old to fear the rod and to cry softly. She didn't say that she spanked them constantly or that they weren't allowed to cry. Instead she taught them to respect authority and exercise self-control as they expressed their emotions. I wish I'd have thought of that "cry softly" bit when my kids were younger! The ultimate goal, she writes, is to conquer a child's stubborn will.

In order to firm the minds of children, the first thing to be done is to conquer their will and bring them to an obedient temper. To inform the understanding is a work of time, and must with children proceed by small degrees as they are able to bear it; but subjecting the will is a thing that must be done at once, and the sooner the better, for by neglecting timely correction they will contract a stubbornness and obstinacy which are hardly ever after conquered, and never without using such severity as would be as painful to me as to the child....And when the will of a child is totally subdued, and it is brought to revere and stand in awe of the parents, then a great many childish follies and inadvertencies may be passed by. Some should be overlooked and taken no notice of, and others mildly reproved; but no willful transgression ought ever to be forgiven children without chastisement, less or more, as the nature and circumstances of the offense may require.[6]

Now that's not exactly the message we get in many parenting books today is it? But Susanna's goal was to teach her children to respect and obey authority. She didn't believe in a namby-pamby, why-bother discipline that leaves kids laughing behind their parents' backs at what they got away with. Discipline was consistent and serious. At the same time, don't miss her heart: *"as would be as painful to me as to the child"*; *"...some (offenses) should be overlooked...and others mildly reproved"*; and *"as the nature and circumstances...may require."* In other words, she's saying it can be painful to discipline our kids, we should ignore some trivial transgressions, go easy on them sometimes, and not overreact. That sounds like a good balance to her discipline. Some fear that slavish obedience will not produce real character. But as Arnold Dallimore writes, "It has been suggested that this principle would make children spineless automatons, yet the

Wesley children grew up to be men and women who showed great strength of character, one of them to a degree superior to almost all others of his time. Susanna trained her children to obey and in so doing she richly moulded [sic] their characters."[7] She raised her children to revere and obey not just their parents, but God.

Her strict routine and rules may not have made her the most fun mom in the world, but I can't argue with her results. Her consistency produced fruit, fruit that I want in my children. And too often I want the fruit without the work. Just about the time I'm ready to say "I don't want to hear another thing about discipline," I'm prompted to learn a few things more from Susanna's example.

Disciplined Devotion: Susanna was also disciplined in her private devotional life. When she was just five years old she decided she would spend as much time in prayer and Bible reading as she did in recreation. She was not your ordinary child. But when she grew up and had her own large family, she discovered what so many of us moms know: Once the babies come, the time for recreation decreases. At thirty she changed her childhood vow, increasing her devotional study to two hours a day. And that was during the period of her life when she was still teaching her children six hours a day! That adds up to eight hours a day, not counting meals, caring for her ten surviving children, and labor-intensive seventeenth-century homemaking (hauling water, lighting fires…). It's enough to make one throw up one's hands and say, "That's it, Susanna. I am from Venus and you are from Mars. This is where you lose the rest of us moms." Thankfully, I came to understand that her discipline style was based upon her tender heart and motivation.

Susanna Was Faithful

The powerful motivation that compelled Susanna to live such a disciplined life was her desire to make certain that her children were true Christians. Her writings reveal that she lived as she did because she was passionate about the souls of her children. That is a passion I share with her. Even though trained in legalism, Susanna had a heart for God and a zeal for spiritual growth. Her passion for God can be seen in her faithfulness to her husband and her children.

Faithful to Her Husband: Marrying a very domineering man didn't make life easy for strong-minded, thoughtful, and independent Susanna. She was also a much better money manager than Samuel. He was in debt his entire life and lacked basic business acumen, making poverty a constant struggle for their family.

Susanna and Samuel also had differing views on politics. One night in 1701, during evening prayers, Samuel noticed that Susanna did not say amen to his prayer for the king. When he asked why, she voiced her opinion that King William III of Orange was not the rightful heir to the throne. Instead, she believed the Stuarts were the rightful line. After calling her to his study he told her, "We must part, for if we have two Kings, we must have two beds."[8] I read that and thought, "Get a grip now, Sam. It's just politics!" But he went further due to his view of submission. He knelt down and prayed for "divine vengeance" on himself and his family if he touched her or shared her bed before she asked for his and God's forgiveness. The next morning he left and stayed away for five months, leaving her to raise the children at home alone. In one of her personal letters she wrote of her concern and added, "Since I am willing to let him quietly enjoy his opinions, he ought not to deprive me of my little liberty of conscience."[9] When the king died, the obstacle of their difficulty was removed and Samuel eventually returned home. The fruit of their reconciliation was their famous son, John.

Samuel was away from home at other times as well. He was thrown in debtor's prison in 1705 and was absent for the next seven winters conducting church business in London. It surprises me that she could endure such a marriage, but Samuel, with all his flaws, had some good qualities too. He desired revival in his parishioners' hearts, and on his death bed he reminded John to "remember the inner witness" for assurance of salvation. In spite of Samuel's dominance, foolishness with money, and even abandonment, Susanna saw the good in him and remained faithful, which blessed their children.

Faithful in Training Her Children: One of the most admirable qualities in Susanna is her commitment to teaching her children. She wanted to be certain they had a deep understanding of Christianity and of life. She struggled to understand each of them as an individual.

One of her teaching methods was to write several manuals on Christian doctrine for her children. They included *A Manual of Doctrine, An Exposition of the Apostles' Creed,* and *An Exposition of the Ten Commandments.* All the time she had spent studying, reading, and thinking began to bear fruit in a form that would bear fruit in her children.

> *We must know God experientially for unless the heart perceive and know Him to be the supreme good, her heart's only happiness, unless the soul feel and acknowledge that, she can have no repose, no peace, no joy, but in loving and being loved by Him.*
>
> —Susanna Wesley

Besides these written "discourses," Susanna left a legacy through letters. She saw that it was part of her role as a mother to continue teaching her children, even after they left home. She wrote about life and God and the way they should live. These were not your typical "How's school going? Do you have any friends?" letters. Some of them are even rather difficult to understand. They reflect her high intellect, her passion for learning, and her heart to train her children. Others are more straightforward. In one letter to Sammy she wrote, "...for I desire nothing in this world so much as to have my children well instructed in the principles of religion, that they may walk in the narrow way which alone leads to happiness." And in another,

"This life is nothing in comparison of eternity;"[10] In a letter to Sukey, who was living with Samuel's brother, Matthew, after their home was burned in 1709, she wrote:

> You have learned some prayers, your creed, and cate-chism....But, Sukey, it is not learning these things by heart, nor your saying a few prayers morning and night, that will bring you to heaven; you must understand what you say....I cannot tell if you have ever considered the lost and miserable condition you are in by nature. If you have not, it is high time to begin to do it, and I shall earnestly beseech the Almighty to enlighten your mind....that you may be his child by adoption here, and an heir of his blessed kingdom hereafter."[11]

One of the things that is very inspiring to me about Susanna Wesley's faithful legacy was the one-on-one time she spent with each child. After reading a book about two Danish missionaries with her daughter, Emelia, she was stirred to consider what else she could do for God. She also wanted to counter some of the negative things her children had picked up when they had lived with neighbors and relatives after the fire, so she decided to spend one hour a week alone with each child. No small task for a household of (at that time) eleven. On Mondays she talked with Mollie, Tuesdays with Hetty, Wednesdays with Nancy, Thursdays with Jacky, Fridays with Patty, Saturdays with Charles, and Sundays with Emelia and Sukey. Susanna wasn't just a rigid "do-it-and-do-it-now" mother. She wanted to know and influence each child as an individual. Instead of being over-whelmed at the scope and consistency of that kind of commit-ment (when I sometimes struggle to give my *four* the attention they need), I looked again at what prompted her action. She wanted to make sure her kids knew the Lord and were growing in their faith. To do that she had to know them. She also did it as an act of service to God. These are reasons I can understand. Her example moves me to invest more individual time with my children so that they will not be found lacking because I chose more leisure time over deeper heart-to-heart discussions with them.

Faithful to God: When Samuel was away during the winter of 1711–1712, Susanna felt obligated to provide the spiritual training that he couldn't provide, so she began Sunday evening services in her home for her children. One neighbor boy told his parents and they came. Then news spread to other neighbors, who began to fill her house to hear her read the most "awakening sermons" she could find. Soon, Susanna's crowds grew to over 200 people in her home. Inman, the curate serving in her husband's place in church, became jealous (her crowds were much bigger than his, or Samuel's for that matter) and he informed her husband. Samuel suggested she get a man to read the sermons, but she replied that there wasn't a man able to read them well enough. He then wrote asking her to stop, but in her reply she explained how people were being touched by the meetings and closed with this great line: "If after all this you think fit to dissolve this assembly do not tell me you *desire* me to do it, for that will not satisfy my conscience, but send your *positive command* in such full and express terms as may absolve me from all guilt and punishment for neglecting this opportunity for doing good when you and I shall appear before the great and awful tribunal of our Lord Jesus Christ."[12] Don't suggest I stop; command me to stop! she said. I love that spunk! She was submissive, but purposeful. As has been written of her, "Her initial passivity, however, turned into a zealous passion to affect spiritual growth among the people who had sought her out."[13] When her husband returned, he found that the parishioners, who had previously been spiritually anemic and hostile to him and his family, had been stirred to amity and growth.

Susanna was faithful to God. She had a plate full of troubles and even struggled with depression, but she remained faithful all through her life. In a letter she wrote to John after Samuel's death, she said of God, "I have long since chosen him for my only good, my all; my pleasure, my happiness in this world as in the world to come...pray for me, that God would make me better, and take me at the best."[14] About a year before she died, Susanna had what John called a conversion experience. She became assured of her salvation simply because of the cross of Jesus, not because of the work she had done for God.

What I'd Love to Tell Susanna Over Tea

Dear Susanna,

You were so disciplined...consistently. You were so faithful...constantly. When I look at my own routine, my own child training, and my homeschooling, I sometimes feel like I'm swimming near the bottom of the food chain. But I have to avoid thinking that way. That attitude comes from comparing myself to you. While we are very different, we share the common ground of a disciplined faithfulness in loving God.

I understand you better when I remember the harsh times in which you lived. People could be jailed for debt, not given an extended credit line. School children's backsides were acquainted with birch rods, not field trips. Water was hauled in, not piped. Too many babies were buried instead of rocked. You had a hard life, didn't you? You were sick and bedridden so often, your marriage was a struggle, poverty was a constant, your family was harassed, and oh...those nine little graves. You were not superwoman; you were a hurting woman who drew strength from God and then lovingly, sacrificially poured your life into your children.

At first I wanted to tell you, "Hey Susanna, lighten up on the legalism and bask in some freedom with me, won't you?" It can be as relaxing as a long soak in a hot tub (and you would have enjoyed that too!). However, God used your methodical ways and your desire for spiritual depth to produce fruit in your children, who then made a lasting impression on the world. And the fruit continues. What a legacy! God made you *who you were* for a purpose. God points me to things in your character that inspire me to be a better mother, while reminding me that like you, He made me *who I am* for a purpose.

Thank you for reminding me that a lot of Christian kids fall away, and I must do all I can to impart deep, lasting, spiritual growth. Thanks for reminding me that helping with school work isn't a substitute for individual time for talking privately with my children. Susanna, it is not your discipline that inspires me, although that is admirable. I am touched, rather, by your heart and your depth. Your zeal for your children's salvation fueled your disciplined faithfulness, and that enabled you to train your children in the way they should go, to sacrifice personal time in order to really know them and to spend time sitting at Jesus' feet to really know Him. That is why you are in my heroine hall of fame.

Sincerely,

Lindsey

TWO

Margaret Ruskin

The Mother of
John Ruskin

1781 – 1871

Look Who Rocked the World

WHO: *John Ruskin*
WHAT: *Writer, Artist, Art Critic, Social Reformer*
WHEN: *1819–1900*
WHERE: *London, England*
WORKS: **Modern Painter, The Seven Lamps of Architecture,
The Stones of Venice,** *and his autobiography,* **Praeterita.**

Many people know John Ruskin as simply "that English art critic," but he influenced far more than the art world. He wielded a great moral influence in Victorian England and helped to shape the thinking of many people including Gandhi, Tolstoy, and Proust. His work consistently extolled the value of beauty and the spiritual values of the Middle Ages.

As a child, his evangelical mother exposed him to the teachings of the Bible. His father, a prominent wine merchant, taught him to love art and romantic literature through evening candlelit read-aloud sessions and extensive family travels. Both parents were devoted to his education because they realized early on that he was a gifted child. Ruskin wrote his first poem at age seven, showed amazing artistic talent by eleven, and published works of poetry and geology by age fifteen. He studied Latin, Greek, and the classics, and he kept copious notebooks of his travels, Scripture study, and other subjects that he taught himself.

Whether Ruskin was writing about art, architecture, science, or social injustice, two things are evident: his love of beauty and the moral and spiritual influence of his early Scripture study with his mother. His beautiful prose is rich with biblical analogies and overtones. As one person wrote "He wanted to teach the world to find the beautiful in nature and in art. He felt it could be found everywhere if only man could be taught to see." Yet he was looking through eyes that had been trained to filter everything through the beauty and principles of Scripture.

Margaret Ruskin

*A Mom Who Faithfully Imparted
the Word of God*

———◦•❖•◦———

"Whatever merit there is in anything that I have written is
simply due to the fact that when I was a child my mother
daily read me a part of the Bible and daily made me learn a
part of it by heart."

—JOHN RUSKIN

———◦•❖•◦———

I grabbed my keys and purse and followed my four
children to the car, or, rather, *herded* them to the
car. "Hurry, children, or I'm getting the cattle prod
out of my purse," I teased. "I call it my Kid-Prod—user-friendly
and use-ee motivating! Now, Collin, do you have your coat?" I
asked.

"Yes, Mom."

"Do you have your vest, Alli?"

"I think so."

"Everyone, do you have your Awana books?"

With one collective "yes" we sped out of the cul-de-sac. It
was Tuesday night and that meant we were headed for two
things: Awana Club and Taco Bell, and not in that order.

"Okay, Claire, could you please turn on the map light and
help your brother go over his Bible verses one more time?" I
asked, wishing I'd spent a few more minutes with him before

tonight's meeting at church. In no time they were juggling tacos and club books while I maneuvered a small burrito and a large Suburban.

"Now, nobody drip beans on your Bibles!" I cheerfully warned.

"Mommy," came little Allison's reply. "I wouldn't do that. Those are God's words."

"I know, and that's exactly what you're putting in your heart."

"Beans?" she asked with wide eyes.

"No, honey, God's words," I replied with a smile.

My children love the Awana Bible memorization club at church, where they have memorized sizable amounts of Scripture in weekly bite-size lessons. They especially enjoy the games that have been invented to help reinforce all that memory work. Our older children memorize independently, then recite their verses to me or my husband, Tim. The younger ones, however, need help. Disciplined help. A variety that sometimes seems in short supply in my own life.

I thought about that as we pulled into the church parking lot. They gathered their things and piled out of the car while I made a mental note to add a few more minutes to each day's study. At least we had improved over years past. The children's bedtime routine included studying their Bible verses and then saying them aloud. Most nights, anyway...

The children went in ahead of me as I stuffed the taco wrappers into a sack. *Margaret would never do it like this,* I thought. Stuff. Crumple. Stuff. *The mother of John Ruskin would never have contemplated last minute cramming as a Bible study method. She was a woman of discipline.* I grabbed the bulging trash sack, slammed shut the car door, and headed for the church, frustrated by my "most nights" approach to Bible instruction as it compared to Margaret Ruskin's "discipline over the years" approach. Opening the front door, I suddenly wished I could sit down with Margaret over tea to learn from this disciplined Victorian lady who had done so well in teaching Scripture to her child.

I first learned of Margaret Ruskin one morning while reading these lines in a Bible commentary: *"Whatever merit there is in anything that I have written is simply due to the fact that when I was a child my mother daily read me a part of the Bible and daily made me learn a part of it by heart"* —John Ruskin.

I was intrigued. Who was this man? What had he written? And my biggest question: What was his mother like? My research led me to an English gentleman who was influenced by a mother with high standards, the discipline to instruct from the Bible, and a dream for her child.

As I temporarily immersed myself in Victorian literature and studied the Ruskin household, I found myself beginning to think in "Victorian English." My internal dialogue sounded like lines from a Jane Austen novel. I would sometimes lapse into nineteenth-century Victorian speech such as, "Our car won't start? Oh, darling, whatever shall we do?" or on Awana nights, "Children, make haste!" It was easy to picture myself in her world, her home…perhaps, according to that fashionable nineteenth-century society pastime, as a social caller.

Just Imagine . . .

**The Southern Outskirts of
London, England, 1828**

I grasped the curved, black-iron railing at the front entrance of Herne Hill and picked up the long, full skirt of my dress just enough to clear the steps. In front of the heavy wooden door I reached in my bag for my calling card, then adjusted my hat and knocked. A servant (who looked amazingly like Anthony Hopkins) opened the door. Handing him my card I said, "Good morning, I am here to see Mrs. Ruskin."

"Do come in please. You may wait in the parlor while I tell Mrs. Ruskin of your arrival," he said with perfect diction and a charming accent. *So this is where he worked after* The Remains of the Day, I mused.

I sat down in the parlor just off the grand center hall and took in the well-appointed room. Elaborate draperies adorned the windows overlooking the garden, and large potted plants were scattered about. A mahogany secretary held a perfectly straight stack of stationery with an inkwell immediately to the right. A basket of embroidery rested near a fireside chair, and on the table next to it was the accompanying thimble, neatly stowed in its case. John James, Margaret's husband, was a wine merchant, so I noticed his silver wine-tasting cup on another table. There was no empty space to be found. On one wall hung a large painting of the young master, standing in a field with a dog nearby.

The massive furniture, heavy draperies, and thick carpeting muffled most of the noises. Silence hung in the air like a cloud, broken only by the ticking of the clock on the mantle. With silent footsteps, I walked over to the tall bookcases and breathed deeply of one of my favorite aromas: the leather of old books. Every spine rested flush with the edge of the bookshelf and I ran my finger lightly along the precise row of volumes. Among the many books I saw *Ivanhoe, Tales of the Castle, Lectures on Rhetoric,* and *Medallic History of Napoleon.* And on one end, *Foxe's Book of Martyrs.*

Hearing footsteps in the hall I meandered towards the door and could just make out a woman's voice.

"Please finish your breakfast, John. Your mother will be ready shortly." *That would be John's nurse.*

"But, Anna, I'm not very hungry today," I heard him reply quietly.

"Young man, your lack of appetite just vexes me," his nurse complained. "Very well then. Straighten your hair before your mother sees you."

A kitchen servant could be heard clearing dishes, then silence. Feeling a bit mischievous, I quietly tiptoed into the hall and peered into the room where they'd just been. All that was left on the table was the child's boiled egg perched in its dish with one bite missing. Next to it rested the egg cup lid, shaped and colored like a chicken.

"Madame?" the Hopkinsish servant said causing me to jump slightly. "Mrs. Ruskin will see you now. Would you kindly walk this way." Thinking of the movie *Arthur*, I resisted the urge to answer, "If you insist," and imitate his gangly stride as I followed him back into the parlor. Seconds later Margaret and her son walked in.

"Mrs. Ruskin, it is so good of you to receive me this early," I said, crossing the room to greet the thin, well-dressed woman. Her pale skin was set off by the few dark curls escaping her bonnet.

"Mrs. O'Connor, I'm delighted at your call," she answered warmly, holding out her hand. "My son and I were just about to begin our morning Bible reading." The boy shyly smiled at me. "Won't you join us? Our guests are always invited to join in, unless you'd prefer to wait elsewhere until we are finished," she said.

"Actually, that's why I'm here," I said. "I understand young John's knowledge of Scripture is vast and that you are an excellent teacher. I would love to observe your methods of instruction, if you and John don't mind."

"We would be delighted, Mrs. O'Connor. Please do," she replied, and motioned for me to join them at the heavy library table. John stooped to stroke the small dog that had wandered into the room. "You know you can't come in here now," he softly spoke to the animal as he scooped him up and placed him out in the hall. John closed the door and joined me at the table while his mother went to the shelf and pulled down a very large Bible.

"Let's begin, shall we?" she said, opening the book between them. "'Rejoice in the Lord always; again I say, rejoice!'"

Without missing a beat John read the next verse. "Let your forbearing spirit be known to all men. The Lord is near." *Ah, Philippians. Now that's familiar.* Margaret read the next verse, then John again, as they continued reading alternately until they had finished the chapter and moved to the first chapter of Colossians. With that done, Margaret sat quietly while John copied several of the verses into his notebook, along with some of his own thoughts. Margaret adjusted her ruffled collar and long pendant, then closed the Bible and looked at John.

"We will pick up the next chapter tomorrow. Now dear, let me hear a bit of the psalm you've been working on," she said. John grimaced ever so slightly, then began to speak. "How blessed are those whose way is blameless, who walk in the law of the Lord," he recited perfectly. I quietly opened the nearby Bible and read along in utter amazement as he said all 176 verses of the longest chapter of the Bible. Every word was right. Every syllable. Every pronunciation. *He knows the whole chapter!* I consciously closed my mouth and tried not to look shocked.

> *"It is strange that of all the pieces of the Bible which my mother thus taught me, that which cost me most to learn, and that which was to my child's mind chiefly repulsive, the 119th Psalm—has now become of all the most precious to me, in its overflowing and glorious passion of the love for the law of God."*
>
> —John Ruskin

"Darling, that was lovely. Well done. One last thing. Let's try again that bit of poetry you were having some trouble with yesterday, shall we?" Margaret instructed.

"Yes, ma'am," her son said obediently, and in the singsong tempo of childhood poetry he began, "Shall any following spring revive, the ashes of the urn?"

"Try it this way dear," said his mother. "The *ashes* of the urn. Place the accent on ashes, not of. You'll find the cadence is much prettier that way." He tried again.

"That was better. We will continue working on it tomorrow. You will master it eventually. Now, do go on to your Latin while I visit with our guest," she said, and we quietly strolled to the other side of the room.

"Won't we disturb him?" I asked.

"Oh, not at all. Excuse me while I tell Mr. Osman to ready the horses and carriage for our upcoming journey," she said. "I'll just be a moment."

I looked over at John and though he had one hand on his Latin book, he appeared to be distracted and mesmerized by something else. Looking in the direction of his gaze, I saw nothing, but his brow was furrowed as if in deep concentration. I retraced his line of sight again, and this time I saw a patch of sunlight falling across the bookshelves and the illuminated dust specks that floated toward the carpet. I watched John's eyes follow one speck until it rested upon the carpet, which he continued to study, tracing the patterns with his eyes.

"John, what do you see in the carpet?" I asked.

"In the beautiful colors and patterns I see a labyrinth of roads and towers and spires," he replied.

"All that?" *What child notices such details?* "What do you like to do when you aren't studying?" I inquired.

"Oh, I love to draw and write poems. I also write my father letters."

"You are quite accomplished for one so young. Well, I'm sorry I disturbed you," I apologized as he quietly turned back to his Latin.

Margaret returned, followed by a servant carrying a tea tray.

"You teach him this way every day?" I asked. She smiled and nodded. "And so much memory work! I am amazed," I confessed. Too often I require far too little of my children."

"Mrs. O'Connor, it is sometimes toilsome, but always necessary." She sipped her tea then gently sat her cup down and leaned forward, smiling as if she knew a very great secret. "You see," said Margaret, "I have a great dream for my son."

Look Who Rocked Ruskin's Cradle

Margaret Ruskin wasn't highly educated, extraordinarily talented, or of noble birth. In fact her father ran a pub. Her impact on the world came not because she was a mover and shaker, but because she was committed to instilling Scripture into the heart and mind of her son. He credited this commitment with making him the writer that he was. Every day from the time he was very small, she read and discussed the Bible with him. They read through it many, many times over the years. But most impressive of all were the many long passages that her son memorized, entire chapters that she had him hide in his heart. By the time he was fifteen years old, John Ruskin knew the Scriptures intimately.

Margaret, a devout evangelical Anglican, was married to John James. He was a successful wine merchant who often traveled on business, but always looked forward to coming home to his loving wife. Margaret was thirty-eight years old when her only child, a son, was born. She saw him as her Samuel, for like Hannah, she had prayed for this child and dedicated him to God before his birth.

She took John to church when he was just two years old (not to the Anglican equivalent of children's church either!) and began educating him when he was very young. Long before curriculum fairs or homeschooling magazines, Margaret Ruskin educated her son at home. In a letter to her traveling husband she wrote: "We get on very well with our reading. He knows all the commandments but the second perfectly and the Lord's prayer. His memory astonishes me and his understanding, too." John was three at the time, the age when his reading instruction began.

Their days had a regular rhythm: breakfast, Bible study, recitations, reading, and then Latin. Afternoons were spent in the garden (John amusing himself while she tended her flowers) or at tea with her husband, and evenings found the boy reading aloud from Shakespeare and the novels of Sir Walter Scott. The exception was

Sunday, when Mrs. Ruskin only allowed the reading of *Robinson Crusoe*, *Pilgrim's Progress*, and *Foxe's Book of Martyrs* in respect for the Sabbath (and to counter Scott's influence!).

The stand-out feature of Mrs. Ruskin's child-rearing was family Bible study, a very common activity for the growing middle class of nineteenth-century England. But Margaret Ruskin's approach to it was uncommon.

Her methods were simple, but intense. Every day after breakfast, she and John read two or three chapters of the King James Bible, taking turns in the reading. She made certain every word and meaning was clear. Then John memorized a few verses.

Simple. No workbooks. No special programs. Just day-by-day work until John was able to recite long chapters by heart, including many psalms, the Sermon on the Mount, and much of Revelation.

One day in John's latter years, while writing his autobiography, he picked up his worn Bible and out fluttered a piece of paper inscribed with the list of his mother's required Scripture memory from his childhood:

Exodus	Chapters	15th and 20th
2 Samuel	Chapters	1st, from 17th verse to the end
1 Kings	Chapters	8th
Psalms	Chapters	23rd, 32nd, 90th, 91st, 103rd, 112th, 119th, 139th
Proverbs	Chapters	2nd, 3rd, 8th, 12th
Isaiah	Chapters	58th
Matthew	Chapters	5th, 6th, 7th
Acts	Chapters	26th
1 Cor.	Chapters	13th, 15th
James	Chapters	4th
Revelation	Chapters	5th, 6th

What a list! Can you picture your child memorizing all of that? Of course, our educational system does not place the kind of emphasis on memorization that previous cultures have, be it Scripture, the names of rivers, or the presidents. Yet experts have found that such mental exercise in the early years, when a child's brain can most easily commit information to memory, yields invaluable and lasting results. It certainly did with John. The results of this study can be seen in his writing throughout his life. Many of us look at that list and think, "Wow, my child could never learn all that." And they can't, not all in one chunk. John didn't either. His achievement came about bit-by-bit, year-by-year, through the encouragement of a very disciplined mother. As Ruskin wrote:

> *In this way she began with the first verse of Genesis, and went straight through to the last verse of the Apocalypse; hard names, numbers, Levitical law, and all; and began again at Genesis the next day. If a name was hard, the better the exercise in pro-nunciation—if a chapter was tiresome, the better lesson in patience—if loathsome, the better lesson in faith that there was some use in its being so outspoken.*[1]

She taught regularly and she worked hard. John recalls "the long morning hours of toil, as regular as sunrise—toil on both sides equal—by which, year after year, my mother forced me to learn these paraphrases and chapters (the eighth of First Kings being one—try it, good reader, in a leisure hour!) allowing not so much as a syllable to be missed or misplaced."[2]

So how did she motivate her son to do this? Gummy worms? Threats? Neither. Here's what John says in his autobiography:

> *This she effected not by her own sayings or personal authority, but simply by compelling me to read the book thoroughly for myself. As soon as I was able to read with fluency, she began a course of Bible work with me, which never ceased till I went to Oxford.*[3]

Two things stand out in that passage. First, John was obedient and bright. She said "read it" and he did, for his own good, not because he was forced. Second, they worked together in biblical study. She didn't pat him on the head as he went up to bed with the admonition, "Now, read your Bible before lights out." Her very presence and habitual discipline became the catalyst. She was a woman who followed through.

When I discovered a volume of the Ruskin family letters, I learned to appreciate another aspect of Margaret Ruskin: her heart. In her letters I found a woman I not only admired, but one I could relate to. Like me, Margaret loved to read and she shared that pastime with her husband. She also loved Scripture, as can be seen in a letter she wrote to him in 1826. She refers to a book she had recently read that she hadn't liked in the past, but now found interesting:

> I only glanced [at] the first volume but all except the mere narrative was new to me and filled with truths of which formerly I had no perception. If this can be the case in human writings how much must it be so with the Bible. Till the Almighty opens the understanding it is a sealed book. When he does [it] is so clear so beautiful that we are struck with wonder with absolute astonishment at our blindness & stupidity.[4]

In her letters Margaret always expressed great love for her husband, as well as writing of typical health concerns, daily family life, and of her pride in John, who looked like "a perfect cherub." It's also clear that she valued God's help in parenting as we can see in a letter written when her son was two years old: "I never met with any child of his age so sensible to praise or blame. This would be dangerous without strong right principles. I pray God to bless our endeavors to instill them and preserve him in mercy to us."

Some biographies, and even some of John's writings, paint a picture of her as a rather rigid woman, very much in control of her very ordered world. But there was also a great softness in her feelings for her child. When he was three she wrote, "I carry in my muff a pennyworth of Captains biscuit which he eats in his walk." And: "I think he grows very fast and he is so good. How impossible it is to tell you what I feel when I look at him. Surely there is no love no other feelings like a mother's towards the first boy when she loves his father."[5]

Across a continent and a span of 170 years, my mother's heart connects with hers.

So, how did she persevere? What was driving her? She had a dream for her son. From the time of her early "prayer of Hannah" dedicating her son to God, her heart's desire was to raise "an ecclesiastical gentleman"—a minister. As clergymen need a solid grasp of Scripture to serve God, she set out to see that he was prepared. She built all her efforts as a mother around fulfilling her original prayer of dedication. This challenged me to put some disciplined actions behind the prayers I had prayed for my own children. Prayers followed by dedicated action. That was Margaret.

But were all her prayer and dreams for naught? After all, John Ruskin never did become a minister. In fact, when he was about forty years old he traded his Christian beliefs for agnosticism, which was reflected in some of his writing for that period. Sixteen years later, though, he returned to a belief in the basics of Christianity. Ruskin, then, demonstrates Proverbs 22:6 in action: "Train a child in the way he should go, and when he is old he will not turn from it."

Margaret's dream for her child wasn't realized in the way she'd planned, but it fueled a discipline that did not come back void. Even though he didn't serve in public ministry, and in spite of his struggles with faith, the Scripture he learned from his mother shaped the man he became. It influenced his writing style and his interpretation of art and literature. It also created a strong evangelical overtone in much of his writing. Her training taught him to read and study Scripture closely, which instilled in him a habit of examining details in all that he did. For his whole life, even the period when he struggled with belief, the Bible was "a limitless source of stimulation, comfort and wisdom,"[6] and he often cited the Scriptures for proof or evidence in an argument or to make a point. The Bible became an indispensible part of his pattern of thinking. As one biographer attests: "None of his experiences in adult life could weaken the effect of the writer's early training." What a confirmation of all his mother's years of effort.

What I'd Love to Tell Margaret Over Tea

Dear Margaret,

How did you teach so much for so long? You could intimidate a person with all your disciplined efforts. To avoid feeling guilty, I find myself tempted to justify. You had servants, only one child (and a gifted one at that), and a naturally rigid demeanor. You were also a product of your culture: a disciplined woman in an age steeped in structure and order. You had separate containers for everything: egg cups, hatbox pin holders, silver boxes for holding stamps, even a dressing table container for collecting hair from your hairbrush! I don't like eggs or wear hats, and I throw my stamps in a drawer. I clean my hairbrush into the trash can.

Like many in your culture, you required a lot from John as you prepared him for Oxford. I recently read that even in early Harvard days, incoming students were expected to know Latin as well as Greek verbs and nouns. They even had to be able to translate any classical author into English. Your example reminds me of how comparatively shallow the intellectual waters are in postmodern America. Our culture prefers videos to Virgil. Despite the fact that we live in different worlds, with different expectations, I choose to resist the temptation to justify myself, reject my guilt feelings, and reach toward the challenge of your example.

Many moms today recognize the need to teach God's Word to our children, but we struggle to keep up the consistency we need in order to motivate our children in this image-saturated society. Sometimes, we simply do not realize that we've set the bar of expectation too low. You keep me from feeling cozy in my shallow water, from patting myself on the back because I remember to help them learn Scripture "most nights." You inspire me to jump into the deep end of all that's available to learn and to teach, and to consistently inspire my children to greater heights than the accepted norms.

I know you realized you made some mistakes. You wrote in your later life that you felt you had overindulged your son. Would you tell me you did all you could do and that John made his own choices in spite of your efforts? Or would you perhaps caution me to balance instruction with developing a deep love for God Himself? Discipline is honorable, and knowledge of the law is indeed a worthy pursuit, but a heart for God is the highest good.

While we are different, we share much, Margaret. You loved the Word of God, your husband, and your son. You valued education and consistent, disciplined instruction. Would you also point me to the strength of the God who stands behind you?

Instead of ordering a pizza and flicking on the remote, you inspire me to turn yet another page in the Bible, press on with one more verse, deliver my children to the next Awana meeting—and eventually, college—fully versed in the beauty and power of Scripture. Whether our earthly dreams for our children are realized or not, God's Word in their lives will always bear fruit. Thank you, Margaret, for challenging me to the high standard of being a mom who faithfully imparts the Word of God.

Sincerely,

Lindsey

THREE

❧

Monica

The Mother of Augustine

A.D. 331–387

Look Who Rocked the World

WHO: *Augustine of Hippo*

WHAT: *The Bishop of Hippo, a scholar, prolific writer, and one of the greatest of the Latin church fathers.*

WHEN: *354–430*

WHERE: *Born in Tagaste, a North African town under Roman rule (present day Algeria). He studied and taught in Carthage (present day Tunisia) and also worked in Rome and Milan, Italy.*

WORKS: Confessions, The City of God

Little did Augustine's mother know when she first rocked his cradle that her son would one day have such a profound influence on both the church and the world. And through his writings, that influence has continued for over 1600 years. Now that's impact! This fourth-century scholar and bishop is considered one of the handful of great Christian thinkers of all time. He wrote more than 100 books, most of which continue to be studied today, along with over 1000 sermons. In fact, more of his writings survive than those of any other ancient writer.

Augustine's most famous work, *Confessions*, is the story of his personal search for God. He confesses his sin as a prideful and immoral intellectual, but also his faith, need, and praise for God. The book is essentially a candid prayer to God, filled with insights for "everyman" regarding sin, God's grace, and the human condition.

Did Augustine rock the world? He certainly did. Some say he is the most influential of all western theologians and "attention to his thought has been one of the constant threads in western intellectual history" whether they agree with him or not.[1] *Who's Who in Christian History* says Augustine was the first to write a self-examination before God using a biblical understanding of man and God's grace *(Confessions)*, and the first to give a biblical view of history, time, and the state *(The City of God)*. He helped establish church doctrine, making "the grace of God in the gospel the theme of theology in the West."[2] Raymond Brown does a fine job of summing up Augustine's impact:

> *Augustine's ministry in an African seaport was to span the world. Well beyond his lifetime his extensive writings were to be read and studied by people in continents and cultures of which he knew nothing. When men and women surrender their lives to Christ, a work begins that lasts for eternity.*[3]

Monica

A Mom of Persistent Intercession

———•◦•———

"She poured out her tears and her prayers all the more fervently, begging you to speed your help and give me light in my darkness."

—AUGUSTINE

———•◦•———

I remember the experience as though it was yesterday. It was my third pregnancy and the baby, my son, was breech. For months the doctor told me, "Don't worry, he'll turn around before long." Every day my husband and I prayed that the baby would decide that head down was where he wanted to be. Instead, his cat-like stretches reminded me that this child had a mind of his own. He liked his lateral "hammock-like" spot and was not concerned that he was making me look like I was carrying a watermelon sideways. But as time began to run out, they scheduled a procedure to try to turn the baby around.

"You're going to do WHAT?" I asked, picturing two doctors playing Twister with the watermelon I was carrying.

"We're just going to press on the outside of your tummy and try to convince your little guy to get where he belongs," the doctor replied confidently. "It may be a little uncomfortable, but it could do the trick." I went home, told my husband, and prayed for the safety of my child and that I could avoid having surgery. My constant prayer became, "Please, Lord, turn this child around."

The day of the "procedure" (don't you just hate that word?), they hooked me up so they could monitor my son's heart rate, and away they went.

They pushed.

They tugged.

They lied.

I suddenly wanted to sit up and yell, "You remember the phrase 'a *little* uncomfortable'? Why don't you guys just reposition my spleen and liver while you're at it? I'm all for creativity, but not with my anatomy!" Then the monitors began to go off. My son's heart rate started to drop. Mine skyrocketed with fear. "Please, God, let my baby be all right." Push. Tug. "Please let him turn." Push. "Please let him turn..." Push "around!"

But he didn't. My son won the tug-of-war. More prayers. More pleading. More questions. "Why, God?" I asked. The Lord chose to answer that question on the day of my son's birth.

A routine surgery in a room filled with cheerful banter between me, my husband, and the staff turned to an eerily silent operating room as they struggled to bring my son into the world. And when they did, my doctor said, "I've never seen this before. Mrs. O'Connor, your son's umbilical cord was wrapped around his neck *five* times!"

In an instant, the words "God's sovereignty" had new meaning for me. Had he chosen to answer my prayers exactly as I had prayed them, my son very probably would have been strangled during the process of a normal birth. Instead, my Heavenly Father, who knows what I need when I do not, answered my prayers in His own way. I am grateful that God is so merciful He does not always give me what I ask for.

There was a fourth-century mother who I know would agree. I met her through the pages of classical literature. She is Monica, the mother of Augustine. Like me, she prayed desperate prayers for her son, but God didn't give her exactly what she prayed for either. While I prayed a simple, yet misdirected prayer for my son's body, Monica had prayed desperate and sometimes misdirected prayers for her son's soul. We both prayed, "Lord, please turn my child around," and, in Augustine's words, "God heard the central point of our longing," and answered—in His own way—the persistent interceding of a mother for her child. Any mother who has ever poured out her heart to God for her child will want to know Monica's story.

Let me introduce you to this woman of relentless prayer by sharing the story of the night of her greatest anguish and most desperate praying. I wonder what it would have been like to have been there, watching her, experiencing this long night with her...perhaps as her servant.

Just Imagine . . .

The Ancient City of Carthage,
North Africa, About A.D. 383

We hurried down a steep hill, and in the twilight I saw the glistening blue-green of the Mediterranean sea and the port for which we were headed. I took a deep breath of the salty, summer air, but there was no time to enjoy the view. I had to walk quickly to keep up with Monica, who was walking quickly, yet cautiously, keeping her eyes on her son who was not far ahead of her. We snaked through the winding streets of Carthage with the young man unaware we were following him.

"Hurry, please," she said to me over her shoulder. "We must not lose him. My son's soul may depend on it!" Her blue eyes shot me a look of determination as she hurried so fast that she didn't even bother to lift her long, linen tunic from the dirty pavement stones.

Monica never took her gaze off him, oblivious to the incredible sights and sounds of this city that had become so prosperous under Roman rule. She didn't care that this international trading city, known for its rich culture and major university, was almost a second Rome. To her it was just a despicable, immoral city of vice where her son had been further enticed into hedonism during his years here studying and then teaching. As for me, I could not help but look at the forums, fountains, and mosaics that we passed and all the people bustling about on their way to the theater or the public baths. I winced as we passed the huge amphitheater. *They say it rivals the great Colosseum in Rome,* I thought, *but I cannot imagine the cruelty of the gladiators' games inside.* I hurried on following Monica, who was following Augustine, as we neared the port.

Suddenly Augustine stopped in front of a ship and began talking with a group of men. Monica hurried to catch up, then ducked behind the corner of a nearby building, occasionally peeking out to watch her son. You could barely hear him at first above the sound of the seagulls and the shouts of the slave masters directing the loading of the ship's cargo.

"Shhhh," she commanded, trying to quiet her own breathing. "I want to hear him."

His companions were facing us, but we couldn't make out their garbled words.

"Let it always be so," he said to the group who laughed heartily in response. "And always seek truth, my friends." Even with his back to us, his clear diction and strong voice reflected his extensive training in oratory. With that he turned and boarded the ship.

"Did you hear him?" Monica asked, smiling for the first time all evening. "He speaks so elegantly. What important positions await him with such fine skills."

"What shall we do now, ma'am?" I asked, as we leaned against the building in the dark.

"We wait. If he doesn't come back soon, I'll go after him. He cannot intend on sailing. He just can't."

"Would that be so bad?" I ventured.

"Terrible! I would lose my influence. He may never become a Christian if he leaves me for Rome!"

She grabbed my arm. "Stay here," she whispered. "I'm going to confront him."

"Augustine!" she called out.

"Mother?" the shocked young man said. "What in the world are you doing here? How did you find me?"

"That doesn't matter. What are you doing? Please tell me you're not planning on sailing," she said.

"Mother, can't you see there's hardly any wind?"

"Then why, pray tell, did you carry your cloak aboard the ship in this heat?" she said, narrowing her eyes.

"It belongs to my friend who is sailing. Besides, no one will be sailing tonight."

"Well, if you do," she retorted, "I'm going with you. I should like very much to see Rome."

"Mother! You cannot possibly be thinking clearly," Augustine snapped out in frustration. "I must get you out of this night air. There is a chapel across the street. Come with me."

With teeth clenched he took his robe with one hand and his mother's arm in the other and walked toward the very building where I stood. I backed up into the darkness as they passed. Then I tiptoed to the corner again so I could hear their voices echoing through the open door.

"Please, Augustine. You have been enrolled from your birth as a catechumen to prepare you for baptism. I only want what is best for you. Rome is so far away. Either you stay, or I'm going with you!"

"Look, Mother. I'll not sail tonight, but I do want to return to my friend on the ship. I told him I would stay with him until he has a fair wind to sail. The ship is no place for you. Just stay here tonight, and I'll come for you in the morning."

"Here?" she asked.

"This place should be a comfort to you, Mother. This is the Oratory of St. Cyprian, where the body of Cyprian was brought after he was martyred a century ago. You know, all of North Africa is being drawn to the Christian faith because of men like him. They say there are more martyrs here than anywhere else in the Roman empire."

"Yes, Son, never forget their sacrifice for Christ."

"Look," he said, changing the subject, "it's quiet here. You can...pray, no doubt." His sarcasm didn't faze her.

"All right....You'll come for me in the morning?" she questioned.

"I shall. Now, Mother, my friend is waiting. Good night." He turned briskly to go, but she caught hold of his sleeve.

"Augustine."

Obligingly, he turned toward her and stiffly accepted her embrace before pulling away to escape into the night, just as he had intended.

As soon as he'd crossed the street and was boarding the ship, I started toward the chapel door, but Monica met me with tears in her eyes.

"Oh, what will I do with him?" she asked, not expecting an answer from me. She watched him through the doorway until he was out of sight.

"What's to become of him?" she repeated as we walked across the stone floor, our footsteps echoing in the silence. "His heart is as cold as these stones. I must pray. I *must* pray. Surely God will answer my prayer this very night." With that she fell onto her knees with her lips moving in silent prayer. In the darkness, I heard her softly crying, occasionally giving voice to her pained prayers.

"Oh, my Lord, please do not let his ship sail tonight," she prayed. "Let him be telling me the truth. You can command the seas, so please, command his ship to stay in its port. My son must not sail. He mustn't," she cried out to God.

I stayed with her as long as I could, then stretched out on the floor for some intermittent sleep. Each time I awoke, Monica was praying. When the first light of predawn appeared, she was on her feet.

"It's nearly dawn. Come with me," she ordered, straightening her tunic. She pushed my hand away as I tried to help tuck her long stray strands of hair back into place. "No time for that. We must find Augustine. I must see if God has heard my cry."

An early morning gun-metal sky met the water where only hours before a ship had been docked. Monica gasped. I watched her twist the drape of her skirt over and over in her hand, staring at the sea in disbelief as we walked to the dock.

"He can't be gone! He lied to me. My God, did You not hear me calling to You all night long to prevent him from sailing? How could You not answer my prayers?" She collapsed onto the wooden pier with deep sobbing. I tried to comfort my normally serene mistress, but she shrugged off my help and clung desperately to the rough wooden railing, as desperately as she had tried to hold onto her son. Her sobs subsided to silent tears as she stared at the sea with the faraway look of a heartbroken mother.

"Monica, remember your dream," I offered, and she sat up a little straighter.

"My...dream," she whispered hoarsely. "It seems so impossible now. He is gone and God did not answer."

"But your dream. And the Bishop's words. They have always given you such hope that your son will return to the faith of his childhood."

"Yes, I have counted them as words from heaven." She sat up and wiped her tear-stained face. "He has heard the name of Christ since I nursed him as a baby. All those years of singing lullabies about our Lord and teaching him as a child...surely my dream will come true. I cannot quit praying. Augustine must come to be a committed Christian." And with that, she rose slowly and headed home to the interior of North Africa, devastated, but nonetheless still praying.

Look Who Rocked Augustine's Cradle

Her name was simply Monica, as most Romans in the fourth century didn't commonly use surnames. This blue-eyed, fair-skinned Numidian woman was born to Christian parents and significantly influenced by a family servant who was a Christian and had been her father's nurse. Monica became a very devout Christian and she married Patricius, a landowner in Tagaste and member of the town council. Patricius was a pagan whose lifestyle showed the lack of a strong moral foundation. After they were married, the newlyweds moved in with Patricius' domineering mother. What a cozy newlywed threesome *that* must have been. I can just imagine the pain of her early marriage: adjusting to a new husband, a pagan household where she was not the mistress, and a mother-in-law who believed lies spread about her by the servants. Yet, Monica became known as a peace-maker. In the face of the tough odds, she was able to win her mother-in-law's affections and see her converted to Christianity. Over time, other women in the town began to come to her for advice in how to deal with an abusive husband, for Monica had gained the respect and love of her harsh, philandering husband, and lived peacefully with him.

You can add to this rough start the pain of miscarriage and still-birth. Is it any wonder that when this twenty-three-year-old woman finally gave birth to her first child, Augustine, she was so filled with joy and dedicated herself to raising him as a Christian? She had another son and one daughter, but neither was as precious to her as her firstborn. Augustine doesn't enlighten us on the details of how he was raised except to say that from the womb of his mother, he was "sealed with Christ's cross." I can just picture Monica rocking and singing songs about Jesus to her baby, creating an oasis of love, faith, and morality in the midst of a turbulent pagan home. But the most prominent aspect of Monica's faith was her devotion to praying for her son. This made an impression that Augustine didn't forget, especially when, at seventeen, he saw his father become a Christian. He knew his mother had prayed for years for this to happen. His father died shortly thereafter.

The family (whose language was both Latin and Punic) was neither wealthy nor poor. They had to make great sacrifices in order to give their son a good education at the University in Carthage, a cosmopolitan city known for learning and culture, but also for the corruption from its brothels and pagan temples. Both parents were dedicated to their son's academic success at all costs and held high ambitions for him. His classical schooling included grammar, logic, and rhetoric (which emphasized language, literature, and oratory). The aim of such a course of study was to produce students who were gifted in their ability to write and able to speak clearly and persuasively. These were skills that Augustine mastered.

I wonder if Monica sometimes regretted the moral cost of his learning. While a classical education has produced many great thinkers and leaders and even today many are returning to this excellent training, Augustine was schooled in a decadent city which affected him. He became associated with friends in low places, was introduced to works of skeptical philosophy and slipped into a carnal life of immorality and pleasure. He moved in with a woman whom he could never marry (because of church and cultural class restrictions) and fathered a child by her. While still maintaining a respect for Christ's name, he became a zealot for the Manichees, a heretical sect, much to the displeasure of his mother. You can imagine her grief. Augustine was bold in his newfound lifestyle and made no attempt to hide any of it, which further drew Monica to her knees for her wayward son. Twice daily, morning and evening, this concerned mother went to church to pray, eyes filled with tears, that she would one day see him become a Christian.

> *"My mother, your faithful servant, wept to you for me, shedding more tears for my spiritual death than other mothers shed for the bodily death of a son. For in her faith and in the spirit which she had from you she looked down on me as dead. You heard her and did not despise the tears which streamed down and watered the earth in every place where she bowed her head in prayer. You heard her..."*
> —Augustine

One night she had a dream that she interpreted as a prophecy from God. She dreamed she was standing on a wooden rule and saw a shining young man coming toward her. He asked what caused her such grief and weeping, and she told him of her persistent prayers for her son's soul. "Rest content," he said. "Where you are, there also is he." Then she saw Augustine standing beside her.

What hope this dream gave her! She held onto it as a promise that her son would one day return to her faith. When she relayed the dream to Augustine, he told her that what it meant was she would join *him*, but she quickly reminded him that the dream did not say, "Where he is, there also are you." Her quick wit impressed Augustine, and he did not soon forget his mother's dream.

However faithful Monica was as a prayer, she was also very good at being a "doer." All her life she tried to be involved in her son's life: his education, his separation from his concubine (with whom he lived for fifteen years), the arrangement of a suitable marriage, and especially the growth of his faith. Sometimes in the midst of all of her praying, her "doing" kicked in and she, like many of us, found herself wanting to help God out a little.

A certain bishop caught her attention. When she found out he was a former Manichee and an excellent debater of heresy, she went to him and begged him to go talk to her son. It went something like this:

"Please converse with my son," Monica pleaded. "I know you can refute his errors and unteach all the ill things he has learned. Then you can teach him the truth."

"Madame, I cannot," the bishop replied. "Your son is as yet unteachable. He is puffed up with the novelty of that heresy. In fact, he's already confused a number of unschooled Christians with his many probing questions. He just loves to debate. It is pointless now. Just leave him alone awhile."

"Oh, but I cannot. Please come speak to him," she implored.

"Be content to pray for him. He is trained in logic and loves to search for truth. If he keeps honestly searching he will find what his error is, and just how wrong he's been," stated the bishop. "In fact, when I was younger, I became heavily involved with the Manichees because my mother was deceived by them. I not only read their beliefs, but I frequently copied out writings from their books. Yet, without ever being told of their heresy by anyone, I eventually saw for myself the errors of their sect and left them. Your son will do the same," he said.

"But I know Augustine will listen to you," Monica pleaded. Then she began to cry, freely letting the tears roll down her face. "Please, talk with him."

By this time the bishop was becoming a bit aggravated that this woman would not accept his answer. Seeing her distress and determination, he concluded, "Go your way, and God bless you, for it is not possible that the son of these tears should perish."

Monica cherished that answer as if it had come directly from heaven, just as she did the message in her dream. Whenever it seemed that all her years of praying were for nothing, she repeated these promises and continued to pray.

Her prayers were being heard, for Augustine went through a long period of doubt and truth seeking, even as he continued to hold onto his worldly pleasures. After deceiving his mother on a Carthage pier, he left for a teaching position in Rome and then in Milan. Monica's seaport crisis represents a timeless truth: that God is able to answer our prayers in ways other than we think to pray. As he later wrote about that time, "But you did not do as she asked you then. Instead, in the depth of your wisdom, you granted the wish that was closest to her heart. You did with me what she had always asked you to do."[4] In spite of his mother's tears, Augustine was sailing toward several people who would be used to bring him closer to God.

Monica later crossed the Mediterranean with her younger son to join Augustine, and when they were together again he told her that though he was no longer a Manichee, he was still not a Christian. He still faced intellectual hurdles to overcome. It would take the Bishop Ambrose's skillful and truth-filled messages and the witness of Christian friends to bring Augustine to the place where he was ready to follow Christ. All Monica's years of persistent praying finally bore fruit when one day, sitting in a garden reading one of the letters of Paul, Augustine realized that they were addressed to him. You can imagine Monica's joy when Augustine told her of his long-awaited commitment to God. What did she do? I'll let Augustine tell you: "She was jubilant with triumph and glorified you, who are powerful enough, and more than powerful enough, to carry out your purpose beyond all our hopes and dreams."[5]

Monica's story ends on a high note. While preparing to return to North Africa with Augustine, they had many sweet conversations and shared a vision of heaven. She told him that now that he was a Christian, she felt her work was accomplished. One week later, at age 56, she died. In Augustine's later writings, he gives great credit to his mother, Monica, "who had for many years wept for me that I might live in Thine eyes," and: "But to you, from whom all mercies flow, she poured out her tears and her prayers all the more fervently, begging you to speed your help and give me light in my darkness."[6] And God did.

What I'd Love to Tell Monica Over Tea

Dear Monica,

   To read your son's writing is to catch a glimpse of you. It is easy to see in him the qualities I've found in you: persistence, single-minded purpose, and a deep devotion to Jesus Christ. Do you remember ever specifically teaching him these things? Wouldn't you love to know when it was and what you did that helped mold Augustine into the great leader of our faith that he became? Was it a night when you explained the concept of God, or pulled him up on your lap and shared from Scripture? Was it the countless nights of lullaby hymns that painted an indelible picture on his heart of a God who loved him and persistently pursued him? Or was it the fact that no matter what he did or where he was, he knew you were always praying for him?

How long is long enough when it comes to praying for our loved ones to find Christ? A year? Five years? Ten years? What would have happened if you had said, "That's it. I've prayed twice a day for fifteen years and I'm done. God must not care." Aren't you glad you continued a few more? How many thousands of prayers does that add up to anyway?

Oh, I know you weren't perfect, but that's a comfort because I'm not either. I don't think you'd mind if I learned from some of your mistakes. If we could sit down over a cup of tea, would you tell me to be careful of too much "hands-on" managerial mothering? Would you caution me to be careful of my son's friends from an early age, as you learned by experience the danger of corrupting acquaintances. Or would you remind me that the pursuit of "the right" education and career path does not necessarily lead to wisdom. Learning and position and influence can be used to serve God, but I know you would tell me that they should never be the goal.

In our results-oriented world we are told that "name-it-and-claim-it" prayers are the way to get answers. Others will cite sacrifice. Others simply pray and walk away. But you inspire me to the discipline of persistent, relentless, untiring prayer. Thank you, Monica, for crossing my path and helping to change the world through your unceasing prayers. And thank you for giving hope to the countless moms who are praying for a lost child to "turn around."

Sincerely,

Lindsey

FOUR

Mary Ball Washington

The Mother of
George Washington

1708 – 1789

Look Who Rocked the World

WHO: *George Washington*

WHAT: *Commander-in-Chief of the Continental Army in the Revolutionary War; presided over the Constitutional Convention, first president of the United States*

WHEN: *1732–1799*

WHERE: *Born at Popes Creek Farm, Virginia; died at Mount Vernon, Virginia*

George Washington, our country's most revered founding father, has been honored and respected for over 200 years as a man of great accomplishment and honorable character. He explored the Virginia frontier as a teenage surveyor and bought land with his earnings. He led Virginia's militia in the French and Indian War. He trained and rallied the Continental Army as their general and commander-in-chief during the Revolutionary War. He presided with dignity over the turbulent constitutional convention, and he unified a struggling new nation as America's first president. As a gentleman farmer he experimented with scientific farming methods and expanded his Mount Vernon plantation to 8,000 acres, making it a successful business. He also directed that his 122 slaves be freed after his death, trained them in various trades to prepare them for freedom, and provided a privately funded pension plan for many slaves who were unable to earn a living.

Washington became a larger-than-life hero in his own day, known not only for his leadership but for his restraint, dependability, courage, honesty, and perseverance. More than a few wanted to make him king, a thought which appalled this mild-mannered, humble man. Thomas Jefferson thought his strongest feature was prudence and said "he was indeed, in every sense of the words, a wise, a good and a great man."

The tall, blue-eyed Virginian was raised to believe in hard work and faith in God, the latter which he did not hide. He prayed daily and encouraged his soldiers to practice Christian virtues. The day after he took command of the army he issued an order "requiring and expecting" his men to refrain from cursing and drunkenness and to punctually attend church services, carrying their munitions with them. On July 9 he wrote, "The General hopes and trusts, that every officer and man, will endeavour so to live, and act, as becomes a Christian Soldier...." He strongly believed in God's directing hand on our nation. When he resigned his commission after the war he said, "As my last official duty, I want to commend the interests of our dear country to the protection of Almighty God. I now take my leave."

Mary Ball Washington

A Determined Mom Who
Instilled Godly Character

"My mother was the most beautiful woman I ever saw. All that I am I owe to my mother. I attribute all my success in life to the moral, intellectual, and physical education I received from her."

—GEORGE WASHINGTON

---

*M*other, please make him stop," my fourteen-year-old daughter complained. I looked up from my grocery list to catch my eight-year-old son leaping down the aisle with outstretched arms and a wide-open mouth. It was hard to tell if he thought he was an airplane or a kangaroo catching flies.

"He's embarrassing me," she continued.

"I can see that. But at least he's having a good time," I replied.

"Mother!"

"Oh, I'm stopping him," I said, quickly steering my cart toward the exuberant child. "Son, gentlemen do not hop or fly in the grocery store. Would you please close your mouth and open your hand." He thought about that a second, then held out his hand, which I quickly took. "Stay beside me."

At the checkout I wrote out my check while my son tiptoed in step to the melodious "Musak."

"*Mom*, he's doing it again," said my teenager. "Quit dancing right now!" she hissed at him.

"I'm not dancing," he defended himself.

I simultaneously grabbed my receipt with one hand, and him with the other, and marched my happy twinkle-toes toward the car. Jacquelyn commandeered the cart, looking around to make sure no one we knew was anywhere near. "It looks like one of you needs to learn about appropriate behavior and the other could be a little more civil," I said.

Not long after that I thought of a paper Jacquelyn had brought home last year: "George Washington's Rules of Civility." I vaguely remembered learning about this list when I was younger. Her paper being long gone, I searched the Internet and found it: *Rules of Civility and Decent Behaviour in Company and Conversation.* It began "Ferry Farm, c. 1744." On my monitor were the beautifully handwritten rules that George had copied into his manuscript notebook for a school penmanship exercise. I printed the 110 rules of gentlemanly conduct and realized this historic document had value for my two grocery-store companions. Particularly twinkle-toes. Lessons on behavior and civility in one entertaining history lesson. What a coup.

"Would you like to learn how George Washington, who was raised on a farm on the frontier, learned how to be a gentleman?" I asked my children, then read them the first rule:

> *Every Action done in Company, ought to be with Some Sign of Respect, to those that are Present.*

"That's the theme for all of these rules," I explained. "Two of the last rules are very important."

> *When you Speak of God or his Attributes, let it be Seriously & [with] Reverence. Honour & Obey your Natural Parents altho they be Poor.*

I finished by reading the last one:

Labour to keep alive in your Breast that Little Spark of Celestial fire Called Conscience.

"Did you know that some of them are even kind of funny?" I asked. I read the second rule:

"When in Company, put not your Hands to any Part of the Body, not usually Discovered."

Suddenly, I had their full attention.

"What does that mean?" asked six-year-old Allison.

"It means don't put your hands under your arms to make that noise," volunteered Collin. Everyone grinned, realizing this was not going to be a boring history lesson.

Run not in the streets, neither go too slowly nor with mouth open, go not shaking your arms, kick not the earth with your feet, go not upon the toes, nor in a dancing fashion.

"Now what does that mean?" I asked.

"It means 'don't do this,' and with much laughter they began shaking, kicking, tiptoeing, and dancing in demonstration.

"That's right," I said. "Especially in the store."

The sixteenth rule fit the moment, so I read:

Do not puff up the cheeks, loll not out the tongue...

The rest of that one was drowned out by laughter while my kiddos puffed their cheeks and stuck out their tongues.

I continued with a serious one.

The gestures of the body must be suited to the discourse you are upon.

"That means don't dance in church," Claire said.

"Well, most churches," I said.

"Or fly in the grocery store," Jacquelyn added.

"You mean, act right in the right place, right?" Collin asked.

"Exactly," I said. They asked for another funny one so I read:

Put not off your Cloths in the presence of Others, nor go out your Chamber half drest.

"What's that mean?" Allison asked, while the older ones cracked up.

"To keep your Winnie the Pooh skivvies under cover," I answered.

That afternoon, when Collin changed shirts in the den, I heard, "Put not off your clothes in the presence of others" from one sister, and "Collin, you are out of your chamber half dressed" from the other. There's nothing like talk of chambers and seminakedness to get your kids' attention. Through laughter, they'd learned a little about civil behavior and how our first president learned these lessons.

Much has been written about George Washington's honorable character and genteel manners, but I wondered what our founding father had gleaned from his mother. Let me offer you a glimpse of how I connected with her as a woman and mother by telling you about an experience she faced when she was just thirty-five. I could envision what it might have been like to have tried to help her during this grievous turning point in her life...perhaps as her friend from a neighboring farm.

Just Imagine . . .

Ferry Farm, Near Fredericksburg,
Virginia, 1743

"Mary, I thought I would ride over and check on you," I said dismounting my horse while balancing a basket on my arm. "How are you doing?" I asked as I looped the reins around the corner railing and climbed the worn porch steps.

"Managing," she sighed through slightly upturned lips, but her sad eyes spoke volumes. "It is so kind of you to ride all this way, but you need not have done that," she replied.

"Well, I wanted to deliver some things that I made for you and the children. Just some corn muffins and ham and a couple of pies. Oh, and the last of my jam from last year."

"That is quite nice," she said as I handed her the basket. She pulled back the gingham cloth and breathed deeply of the scent of smoked ham and sugary apples. "Mmmm. I am very much obliged." She smiled as she sat the basket beside her. The wind blew the ties of her slightly starched cap and picked up the edge of her wrinkled black mourning dress. Sitting in the rocker next to her, we looked out to the Rappahannock River before us. Her rocking chair creaked on the wooden porch boards and a horse whinnied in the distance.

"Mary, the service was lovely. So many people came from so far away to attend—some as many as thirty miles," I said.

"So true. Gus would have been greatly shocked."

"The Reverend honored Gus well, I believe....Tell me, though, have you slept much since the funeral? You look so distressed and exhausted," I inquired, noticing the dark circles of fatigue and grief ringing her eyes.

"I suppose I've slept as well as could be expected. Well...actually I have been very unwell. I feel like this is the first time I've sat down since he died." Her eyes were still on the river. She turned her head toward me as if she'd just registered that I'd arrived. "Look at me. Here I sit and it is not even the Sabbath. How strange."

"But, Mary, you have been through so much."

"It is odd. I keep expecting to see him hunched over his books at his desk figuring his accounts for this plantation." Her voice trailed off and her eyes glistened. "He may have traveled a great deal managing his ironworks, but when he was home he loved a country dance," she reminisced softly with a smile.

"Yes, he was very graceful in the drawing rooms."

"Listen," she said, "I was thinking it might be a good idea to ride around the plantation and see what I have in store for me now that I am its mistress. You are welcome to ride along."

We mounted our horses and headed around the house. "George," she called to her eleven-year-old son as he walked out of the stable. "Keep watch on the boys. I shall return before dark."

"Yes, ma'am," replied George immediately. Five-year-old Charles and seven-year-old Jack were playing with sticks in the dirt, unaware of the tension on the farm. Sam stood nearby wavering between joining them or doing something more appropriate for a nine-year-old boy who'd just lost his dad. Bet, Mary's slave inherited from her mother, hung up freshly boiled laundry while ten-year-old Betty watched. Sam and Betty knew that life had just changed drastically and were doing their best to lay low.

As we began the long ride across her tobacco farm, I looked back at the five children and suddenly saw the reality of Mary's need to learn quickly how to run a plantation.

"Mary, I trust you plan to hire an overseer, do you not? You cannot possibly run Ferry Farm alone?" I ventured as our horses plodded along in the dirt.

"No. I cannot afford such an expense. Gus may have owned thousands of acres, but he was land poor. Most of that has now gone to Lawrence, as expected. When Gus and I became engaged, my guardian, George Eskridge, advised me of this English law. I knew full well that the lion's share of a father's estate goes to the oldest son, but who thinks about inheritance laws when you're in love. Besides, Ferry Farm has been quite adequate for our needs and has the sweetest well water anywhere."

"Mary, would you do it again?"

She got a distant look in her eyes and sighed. "Most definitely," she said with conviction. "The last twelve years with Gus have been wonderful. I shall miss him so very much. We loved this place, you know. And George will inherit all 260 acres of Ferry Farm when he comes of age." We rode in silence for a while, scanning the less than fertile fields from which she would have to coax a productive crop in order to survive.

"Mary, do you have any idea how to grow and market tobacco?" I asked as we made our way across the field.

"Well, I certainly didn't have my eyes closed all these years. I know I shall have to check the plants for disease, cut them when ripe, and hang them in the curing sheds to dry. Then it must be loaded into hogshead barrels for the warehouse, where Gus' factors will ship it to England and then pay me." I looked at her wide-eyed, imagining all that work and beginning to admire her determination.

Mary stopped her horse and gracefully dismounted. "We must all work harder now." She stroked the velvety nose of the horse she'd been riding. "Hero, you may even be forced to become a work horse. That would certainly sadden George now, would it not? You were a gift from his father." Hero snorted and she turned from the horse, letting the reins fall slack. I saw a storm brewing in her eyes as she looked out at the waiting fields. Then she knelt down and picked up a handful of the worn-out dirt. It sifted through her fingers and blew into the wind. "Gone. Just like that. One minute I held him, the next he was...gone," she whispered as she held out her dirty, empty hand. "Whatever shall I do? I loved him so." Tears began to stream down her face. "I shall never again have the pleasure of his companionship, his love, his strength. What shall I do without him?"

I went to her and silently put my arm around her as she sobbed. Under a gray sky we knelt in the dirt out of view of the children and servants—me trying to comfort, her trying to come to grips with the devastating turn of her life.

Her crying subsided to silent tears as she clasped her hands and began whispering the Lord's prayer and Psalm 23. Visibly strengthened, she wiped her eyes, leaving streaks of dirt on her face.

"I will just have to add farming to spinning and weaving and soap-making and candle-making," she said.

"You must ask for help from your family," I offered.

"And subsist on charity? Never! The Lord will provide." She pressed her lips together and stood up.

"But, Mary, have you considered letting some of your relations take in the children for a time? That way they would be well cared for and fed while you..."

"Nonsense. Lawrence has already offered. He is quite taken with George, you know. They are becoming fast friends." She wiped the dirt from her face with her petticoat. "He wants George to live with him at Mount Vernon. He's a fine young man like his father and I know he will be an excellent example for George...down the road just a bit." She quickly brushed the dirt from her skirt. We mounted the horses and rode back toward the house.

"I *have* to learn to make this tobacco profitable, even if Gus found that difficult while running his ironworks as well." She clenched her teeth and looked at me with determination in her blue eyes. "I have no other choice," she said with resolve, then coaxed her horse into a gallop.

Once at the barn, Mary dismounted and handed her reins to a servant. He looked at me.

"You be stayin' tonight, ma'am?" he drawled as his dark, weathered hands took my reins.

"No. Thank you. Keep her saddled; I am leaving soon."

He led the horses into the barn as Mary and I walked back into the house.

"Mary, if there is anything I can do to help with the children..." I began.

"They shall be a help to me."

"Yes, but..."

"And so will these." She walked to her secretary and picked up a book entitled *Contemplations*. "I know I must become a plantation mistress, but I shall also teach my children character..." then she paused as she slid her hand along the cover of her well-worn family Bible "and faith. It is my duty."

Look Who Rocked George's Cradle

My first clue to the depth of Mary Washington's influence was found in a book written in 1878 that describes many of the "distinguished men of our country," including Washington, as having been raised in remote places by women on the American frontier. The author says, "They drew in with their mother's milk the intellectual and moral traits, and gathered from their mother's lips those lessons which prepared them in after years to guide the councils of their country in the most trying period of its history."[1] It pointed me to a 1676 book that Mary Washington owned and read to her children entitled *Contemplations, Moral and Divine* by Sir Matthew Hale. "A precious document! Let those who wish to know the moral foundation of his character, consult its pages."[2] So I did. But before I share that, let me share what else I found out about Mary Washington.

I soon discovered that there is a great deal of disagreement among historians about the relationship between Washington and his mother. Unfortunately, primary source documents on Mary are scarce.

We know a great deal about George Washington because he wrote thousands of letters and kept diaries, activity journals, expenditure records and other documents, which are contained in some ninety volumes—more than any other president. However, there are few of his mother's records and he didn't write any memoirs concerning her, so there's little primary evidence to unequivocally explain the relationship Mary had with her son. With all of Washington's writing, how I wish he had shared these insights in the way Ruskin did.

If you read most of the modern secular writings about her, you will see her described as a controlling, demanding, possessive, meddlesome, embarrassing mother who became preoccupied with a fear of poverty in her latter years and had a troubled relationship with George most of his life. However, if you read the nineteenth-century writings you will find a far kinder, gentler view of their relationship and glowing, flattering accounts of the mother of the father of our country. So which view is correct? Are last century's writings about her accurate or are they romanticized efforts to retain the sparkling image of our first president? Are this century's writings correct or are they the work of overly critical modern revisionist historians? The older works don't reveal her flaws, and the newer ones rarely touch on her strong Christian faith.

Mary Ball Washington was born at Epping Forest in Lancaster County, Virginia in 1708. She was the only child of her father's second marriage, and he died when she was only three. Her mother remarried, but when Mary was thirteen she was orphaned. From her mother she inherited linens, pewter, dishes, some furniture, and one slave, as well as her affinity for horses and a devout Anglican faith. George Eskridge, a family friend and her mother's executor, became her guardian and she went to live at Sandy Point in Westmoreland County. Mary grew to love the outdoors, flowers, and, eventually, Augustine Washington. Unlike most colonial girls of that time who were wed between sixteen and eighteen, she didn't marry until she was twenty-three—and then to a widower fourteen years her senior, a man with three children. Neither the instant family nor warnings about English inheritance laws could dissuade Mary from marrying "Gus," the love of her life.

One year later, in 1732, George (probably named after her guardian) was born at Popes Creek Plantation. She had five other children: Betty, Charles, John Augustine ("Jack"), and Samuel, as well as a baby who died. Of course there were also three stepchildren: Lawrence, Austin, and Jane, but the boys were away at school and never lived with them, and Jane died at a young age. All her children no doubt understood the hard work of colonial farm life, but George, as her eldest, especially experienced this reality when his father died. He was only eleven. Instead of going to England for his education, like Lawrence and Austin had done, he made do with his seven or eight years of schooling so that he could help his mother with the farm and become the new "man of the house." Mary allowed George to spend a great deal of time with Lawrence, who was able to add to his education and introduce him to society through the Fairfax family (Lawrence's in-laws). Mary's iron will enabled her to make a success of the tobacco business, raise her children alone, and keep their family farm.

When George was fourteen and had been living at Mount Vernon with Lawrence for a year, he packed his trunk, then asked his mother's permission to become a midshipman in the British Navy. Doubtful of the plan, Mary sought the advice of her half-brother in England, who advised against it. On hearing his reasons, she expressed to George her displeasure with the idea. Disappointed, George honored his mother's wishes.

Instead of joining the Navy, George joined a surveying expedition for Lord Thomas Fairfax, Lawrence's influential father-in-law. This marked the beginning of George's career and allowed him, even as a young man, to begin to acquire land with his wages.

When George later joined the Virginia Militia, this didn't exactly thrill his mother. Some interpret her objections to his soldiering as meddlesome, but I think mothers across the centuries can identify with the pain of seeing their beloved son risk his life in a dangerous job. Concerned for him, and unimpressed by his quick advancement, she just wanted him safely out of military service. It seems she even visited him once at an encampment "alarm'd with the report" of his attending General Braddock.[3] Another source cites George's response to his mother's objections during that visit. "The God to whom you commended me, madam, when I set out upon a more perilous errand, defended me from all harm, and I trust he will do so now. Do not you?"[4]

George went on to serve with General Braddock, and a month after his mother's visit George wrote a short letter beginning with "Honoured Madam," a phrase he used in every letter he wrote to her. He closed with "I am, Honour'd Madam, Yr. Most Dutiful and Obedt. Son." Some suggest this shows a cold, unaffectionate relationship between a frustrated son and a meddling mother and have interpreted the formal tone he maintained in his letters to her through the years as anger or intentional distance. However, is it not more simply explained as a reflection of the formality of their culture or a continuation of the formal tone George used so often in his prayers and other writings? He may have simply been honoring his mother as he'd been taught.

Of the few letters that Mary wrote, there are two that she would probably have never sent had she known they would be used by some as public evidence of her character flaws. Over 200 years later, they are even mentioned in a children's biography of her.

In one letter she wrote to George while he was away serving General Braddock and asked for "a Dutch man" (a German farm manager) and "some butter." Not a good move. Here was her son far from luxury in a military camp. It wasn't exactly like he could run up to the nearest 7–11 store for some margarine. George casually and formally replied from his army post that neither were to be had on the frontier.

And yet George was a manager involved in the details of his farms. When he was commander-in-chief, with the weight of the new nation's survival on his shoulders, he wrote very specific letters to his farm overseers about crop rotations, livestock care, and planting hedges instead of building fences. So it is quite possible that his mother knew of his gift with details and told him some of her specific needs. He might have had an answer. In this case he did not.

Her most infamous letter was over money. When she was in her sixties and could no longer maintain Ferry Farm, George moved her to a house he bought for her in Fredericksburg, near her daughter Betty. He appointed his cousin to oversee Mount Vernon and his mother's financial needs while he was away during the ongoing rebellion. However, Mary became concerned. After almost five years of George's absence, seeing her son-in-law, Fielding Lewis, almost fall into bankruptcy by manufacturing weapons for the Continental Army without pay, and not wanting to be totally dependent on her children, she wrote a letter to the Virginia Assembly. As the mother of four sons in the war, one of whom was a general, she felt entitled to a little assistance and asked them for a pension explaining that "I am in great want…" Any wealthy, prominent political leader today would be appalled at having his mother publicly ask the government for a handout. So was George. Embarrassed, he ended the matter with a reply to the Assembly saying he was "confident …that she has not a child that would not divide the last sixpence to relieve her from *real* distress" and that "in fact, she has an ample income of her own." Many historians point out that shortly thereafter he rode right through Fredericksburg and did not stop to see her. While this is true, it should not be forgotten that he was in the midst of commanding the brilliant forced march at Yorktown. On his return, he escorted his mother to the Victory Celebration Ball.

As a patriotic leader who was dedicated to his troops, George suffered as they did (including the bitter winter at Valley Forge) and only went home for approximately ten days during the entire eight-year war for independence. For seven years of the war, he did not have any contact with his mother. Patriotism or anger? It is open to interpretation. Yet, before the war he had provided a house for her near her daughter Betty, who could care for her, and he hired an overseer for her beloved Ferry Farm.

In 1787, in his longest surviving letter to her, George writes that he doesn't want to be viewed as an "unjust and undutiful son," and in his typical formal tone assures her that "I do not mean by this declaration to withhold any aid or support I can give for you; for whilst I have a shilling left, you shall have part, if it is wanted, whatever my own distresses may be."[5]

Do you find yourself both questioning and liking Mary? I did as I studied her. But if we are going to judge her by anecdotes and documents open to differing interpretations, we must also view her in light of her culture, George's statement of her influence in his life, and the nineteenth-century historians who point to her faith and habit of daily prayer, attributes she passed along to her son. She's in this book, flaws and all, because like the rest of us she was a Christian mother determined to train her children in godly character, and the results of that training were evident in George.

Whatever the relationship between Mary Washington and her son, he is still on record as crediting her influence for all that he became and her moral education for his success. So how did she do that?

> *"My son, neglect not the duty of secret prayer."*
>
> —Mary Washington

Since George never told us, and Mary wasn't much of a writer, we have few details about how she trained her son. One nineteenth-century writer said she was an earnest and devoted Christian who strove to "glorify God as much in the rearing of her children as in the performance of any other duty."[6] Another wrote: "In addition to instruction in the Bible and Prayer Book, which were her daily companions, it was Mrs. Washington's custom to read some helpful books to her children at home, and in this way they received much valuable instruction."[7]

One of those helpful books was *Contemplations, Moral and Divine,* the volume some said was her favorite. It contained devotional writings on topics including "Of Wisdom, and the Fear of God," "Of the Knowledge of Christ Crucified," "Of Humility," and "Of the Redemption of Time," among others. It also contained a beautiful letter of advice from the author, written to his children. In reading *Contemplations,* I saw lessons in moral and godly character that Mary valued. It's also easy to see many of these same traits in the character of George Washington. Others agree: "Those who are familiar with the character of Washington will be struck, on reading these *Contemplations,* with the remarkable fact that the instructions contained in them are most admirably calculated to implant and foster such principles as he is known to have possessed."[8] Of those traits another author added, "They certainly were exemplified in his conduct throughout life."[9]

What I'd Love to Tell Mary Over Tea

Dear Mary,

What a roller coaster life you led—from being orphaned to marrying your love, from being widowed to being the mother of our first president. Through it all, you had the determination to persevere. I can just picture you as a bride exploring your new home, which Gus had previously shared with his first wife. Instead of fighting her memory, you made your mark. When you picked up *Contemplations* and saw the inscription "Jane Washington," you just dipped your quill in the ink and added "And Mary Washington."

As I read about your possessiveness and complaining, I try to picture you against the backdrop of your colonial world. You were expected to marry young and have a large family to help with the work of producing most of your goods at home. Death was common, and smallpox and typhoid claimed the lives of a third of the children under three. When the average life span was about forty, it's no wonder you were possessive about your children. Yet you still sacrificed to allow better opportunities for George. With money scarce during and after the war, and much trading done in tobacco, it's easier to understand your financial worries in an age when all property and money were managed by husbands (or grown sons for most widows). Yet in an age of little education and high female illiteracy, you could read. Good for you, and good for George.

I empathize with what you must have gone through when Gus died. You were just thirty-five, had five children, and had to learn to run a plantation. I saw thirty-five a few years ago, have four children, and cannot imagine depending solely on my small garden for produce without some supplemental help from Safeway. Some say you grew tough and domineering. Would you say you had to in order to survive? Some say your children never dared cross your harsh temperament. I say it's no wonder you struggled with impatience after an exhausting day, sitting down to a meager dinner with five tired, fatherless children. Besides, both you and Gus believed in requiring obedience from your children. I think that being robbed of your parents in adolescence and widowed young certainly shaped your independent strength and will.

Yet, I can picture you with dirt under your fingernails and the sweet scent of green tobacco on your gingham dress, gathering your young brood around you saying, "Come here, children. Quiet now. Let Mother read to you." And from the pages of God's Word and *Contemplations* you found the strength and guidance you needed to instill faith and character in your little ones.

How you loved a simple, independent life. It's no wonder that you never cared for Mount Vernon or liked entertaining George's important, cultured friends in their silk hoop skirts, uniforms, and powdered wigs. At Ferry Farm you could stay in your gardening dress all day if you wanted.

When I see the flaws that some biographers point to, I see that even our imperfect mothering can be used by God. Perhaps George would say that despite difficult family relationships God can use us for His service. Perhaps you'd point out that we can be and think differently than our children, and perhaps even have a difficult relationship with them, but God will always honor the investment of godly character training. Despite the differences between you and your child, you valued him. You didn't always see eye-to-eye, but you didn't let that stop you from being involved in his life. Even if we don't endorse the product or process of our children's lives, we can value the person, can't we, Mary?

Some of the qualities for which you are criticized are the very qualities that made your son a great leader. You were called stern and commanding. Those qualities in him made him a general. You were tenacious and determined in the face of fear and obstacles. Those qualities in your son helped him unify a struggling nation. You were intent, frugal, and diligent as he was. You were a praying woman of faith who raised a son who became the leader of our nation founded on the principles of that faith. For that I not only admire you, I thank you.

When I struggle to meet the needs of a child so different from me and am tempted to tell God that He assigned my child the wrong mother, I think of you and remember that we were both chosen for *our* children. Whether I'm instructing my children with *Rules of Civility* pantomimes, offering them new insights from old "contemplations," or just teaching as we walk along the way, I desire to be a mom who instills godly character in my children, just as you did.

Sincerely,

Lindsey

FIVE

Jochebed

The Mother of Moses

c. 16th Century B.C.

Look Who Rocked the World

WHO: *Moses*

WHAT: *Egyptian prince, Hebrew emancipator, leader, lawgiver, prophet, servant and scribe of the Lord*

WHEN: *1526–1406 B.C. (according to the biblically conservative view of dating)*

WHERE: *Land of Goshen, Memphis, Egypt (near present day Cairo), Midian desert*

Whether it be from children's picture books or deMille's movie *The Ten Commandments* or the movie *The Prince of Egypt,* almost everyone knows the story of Moses. He took an enslaved people, executed the most dramatic emancipation in history, then led, organized and administrated their vast numbers, delivering them to the threshold of their promised inheritance. He was the greatest figure of the ancient world and a foreshadowing of Christ; both were prophets, priests, kings, miracle workers, and deliverers.

Moses was raised by both his Hebrew mother and his adopted Egyptian mother, the Pharaoh's daughter. This combination gave him an identity with his countrymen and God, as well as providing the best Egyptian upbringing available—that of a prince. He was highly trained intellectually, socially, and militarily, and lived the rich life of the adopted grandson of the pharaoh. He served in military leadership for his adopted country, which was wealthy and culturally advanced (thanks to the help of Israelite slaves). Even though Moses was an heir to the Egyptian throne, he rejected wealth and power and the highest office of the land. God had placed a passion for His people in Moses' heart, a passion so strong that it led to murder when he saw a slave mistreated. Fleeing to the desert of Midian, he lived in relative obscurity as a shepherd until, at eighty years of age, the reluctant Moses was called by God to be the deliverer of the Israelites.

Moses was humble, never wanting glory or power for himself. His courage was matched only by his extraordinary faith. With total trust and firm obedience, he allowed God to empower him to deliver his people.

A.W. Pink points wonderfully to the antitheses of Moses' life:

> He was the child of a slave, and the son of a queen. He was born in a hut, and lived in a palace....He was the leader of armies, and the keeper of flocks. He was educated in the court, and dwelt in the desert. He had the wisdom of Egypt, and the faith of a child....He was backward in speech, and talked with God....No man assisted at his funeral, yet God buried him.[1]

With simple faith in God, Moses rocked the world.

Jochebed

A Mom Who Faced Fear with Faith

"I sought the LORD, and he answered me; he delivered me
from all my fears."

—PSALM 34:4

My southern roots showed in my cooking. I
stirred the pinto beans, took the cornbread
out of the oven, then added the last touch to
the meal—whole green onions. Mmmm. It smelled good. It was
Saturday and I was enjoying my first-year-of-marriage-I'm-
learning-to-be-a-wife homemaking thing. Up to now, I'd had
little time for homemaking due to my job at a local television
station. *This isn't as much fun as anchoring a broadcast, but it's a lot
more fulfilling,* I thought, surprised at the change in me since
discovering I was pregnant. That made it all the more fright-
ening when I began to suspect that something had gone wrong
with my pregnancy.

Tim came in from running errands one afternoon and found
me full of fear. "There's something really wrong with the baby!"
I sobbed. He reached for the phone to call the ambulance but
decided he could get me there faster. Before he carried me to the
car, my strong, young husband put his arms around me and
said in a shaky voice, "God will take care of this baby. And then

we'll have lots more." After calling my parents to have them meet us, he raced me to the hospital, carried me into the emergency room and, while waiting for the doctors, he sat down in the hall next to my parents. My mom put her arm around him as he wept for the unborn child that he had just realized he loved.

A little while later, the doctor on call had him join me in my room.

"Mr. and Mrs. O'Connor," the doctor began, "you have not lost the baby, but things are very precarious. It's called an attempted miscarriage..."

"But I didn't do anything..." I protested.

"I know. We just discovered you have a condition called *placenta previa*. There's nothing more we can do for you now, so we're letting you go home. But you must remain in bed. And I must warn you that there is a fifty-fifty chance you will lose this baby later tonight."

A little later I was settled on the sofa at my parents' house, much closer to the hospital than our own apartment. Their house was quiet again, and Tim slept nearby in the recliner. *Tick. Tick. Tick.* The grandfather clock ticked off the minutes as I lay motionless in the dark. Waves of fear for my unborn child mixed with memories of what other doctors had said months earlier.

> *"Is my child going to die tonight? Please God, no!..." How had my conversation with that first doctor gone?*
>
> *"Mrs. O'Connor, you are pregnant."*
>
> *"But I can't be."*
>
> *"Well, you are. Unless, you care to terminate the pregnancy. I'll have my nurse talk to you about that on your way out."*
>
> *"That won't be necessary."*

Then the conversation two months ago with my new obstetrician floated across my consciousness.

*"The two medications you have been taking while unaware
you were pregnant could cause a birth defect."*

"I know. I've already been offered an abortion. No thanks."

*"That's not what I'm offering at all. I've seen God work
miracles."*

I remembered leaving his office excited about the child within
and the miracle awaiting us. The crashing waves of fear began
to subside into little lapping waves of uncertainty. I suddenly
realized I might have to stay in bed for weeks or months to keep
from losing this child.

*What about my job? Guess we'll just have to set up a live-shot
in my living room. "Welcome to Newsline 10...live from my
sofa...." Yeah, right. The TV job will have to go. I'll have to...
quit. What if I have to stay in bed for the next five months? I
should have taken Basket Weaving 101 in college. That would
come in handy about now. Maybe I can pass the time by
drawing. Wait. I draw like a three year old. I may still
remember how to knit. Yeah, I can knit....Wait. I hate to knit.*

I fingered the soft "afghan in progress" that my mother was
making for her first grandchild, cleared my crazy thoughts, and
turned for comfort and help to my Heavenly Father. And in the
still of the night I heard Him say, "Do you trust Me?"

*Yes, Lord, I trust You. I have to trust. But this is scary. My baby
might die tonight! That's the only thing that matters right now. Lord,
only You know if my baby will ever live to use this little blanket. If
it does survive tonight, he or she could be born with something ter-
ribly wrong. Please save our baby. We need a miracle.*

We got one. God carried my baby through the night, and after
a pregnancy involving lots of bed-rest, we had a healthy girl.
Today that baby is our beautiful teenager, Jacquelyn.

As I think back on that fearful time I realize that it was only in the arms of my Heavenly Father that my waves of fear began to ebb. Faith began to grow. And that night I knew that, like Moses' mother, I had to bring my baby to the Nile...and let God save my child. In the river of my mind and the still of the night I released my baby to God's protection. I was powerless, but He was powerful.

Jochebed also struggled with fear for her unborn child. Her baby was in danger long before she neared the Nile. She had good reason to fear for her baby's life while she was still pregnant. Did she feel like me? I could see myself with her the last night of her pregnancy, anguish over her coming child. It was easy to picture myself there...as, say her Hebrew midwife...

Just Imagine . . .

Northeast Egypt, the Home of
Jochebed and Amram, 1526 B.C.

"Amram, are you in there?" I called through the doorway. I knocked again and a girl, approximately nine, opened the door.

"You must be the daughter of Amram," I said.

"Yes, I'm Miriam," replied the dark-eyed girl. "Are you the midwife?"

"Yes, I understand your mother's hour has come." She quickly ushered me into their four-room house. It was like so many in the neighborhood with its stone foundation, mud-brick construction, and wooden stairs. But this one was smaller than most. The girl led me through the open air courtyard where a little boy was playing a game with pebbles.

"Is that your brother?" I asked.

"Yes, that's Aaron. He's three. Follow me, my mother is up here," she said, putting her foot on the bottom rung of a wooden ladder. "It's a little messy. We mostly use this area for storage."

"My dear, I am used to that by now. I usually deliver babies in these upper rooms. How is your mother doing?"

"I think she's nearly ready for you." She called out as she reached the top of the ladder, "Mother, the midwife is here! I'm going back to Aaron and the bread-making. If you need me just call." She smiled at me with gratefulness as she squeezed by me and descended the ladder.

"How are you, Jochebed?" I asked as I looked her over. Droplets of sweat trickled down her temples and the hair framing her face was damp.

"Ready to be delivered," she said wearily. I thought of the field I passed on my way here, where our fellow Hebrews were slaving under the Egyptian taskmasters, and couldn't help taking note of the irony in her comment.

"Well, let me see how close you are. May I call for Amram to bring the birthing stool from my cart?"

"Yes, he is on the roof."

I climbed a second ladder and saw Amram on his knees. I hated to disturb a praying man, but when he saw me, he rose. I asked for his help and he practically ran across the rooftop, but before he descended the ladder he turned to me. "You know, my wife does not know what kind of person you are. She has heard rumors of Pharaoh's secret order for midwives to only allow female babes to live. Are you to break her heart tonight if she should have a son?"

"Amram, fear not."

"She also knows of a new edict to take baby boys and drown them in the Nile," he said gravely.

"Of that I can only say that we must pray. I must go to her now."

"Thank you. May God be good to you in return," he said softly, then he hurried to bring in the birthing stool. I returned to find Jochebed, who was leaning forward, gripping the edge of the wooden table next to her. She grimaced and her knuckles whitened as another contraction swept over her.

"It won't be much longer now. You're doing great…" In her eyes I saw fatigue, and pain, and fear. I knew I could do something about the fear.

I pushed her hair out of her face and said, "Amram has told me that you are aware of the plight of newborn Hebrew boys." She looked at me with wide eyes and began to breathe deeply, deliberately. She took the cup of water from me with trembling hands.

"I have had many months to ponder the fate of my child. When Miriam was born it was sheer joy. And Aaron was born just before Pharaoh hatched his demonic scheme. But with this child… I have lain awake at night wondering, imagining the worst, and hoping that my God will deliver. Much is in your hands tonight. I have waited months to know the outcome." She scarcely whispered the last.

"My dear Jochebed. I am very aware of Pharaoh's wishes, but you can trust me. I and most of the other midwives fear God *far* more than we fear what the king would do to us! We have not openly defied him, but if you should have a son tonight, rest well; no harm will come to him by me." Jochebed sighed, and tears began to run down her cheeks.

"Bless you," she cried, burying her face in her hands. "I have prayed so long!" Then another contraction came…and went. "You know," she said after she'd caught her breath, "in the dark of the night when the house was quiet and all I could think of was this child, I went over and over my options. Perhaps I would have a girl. But the only thing I could see was a boy and that made my mind reel. I wondered if my midwife would obey her orders and kill my son as she birthed him. Then I thought, no, maybe Pharaoh will change his mind and rescind his order so my son would not be in danger."

She sipped some water and I wiped her face with a cool rag. "Then," she continued, "I heard of his insane new edict to murder the newborn boys, and I had to repeatedly fight back the image of his guards coming to my house and ripping my baby son from my arms so they could march down to the Nile and throw him to his death."

"Don't forget, God is mightier than they."

"That is the thought I cling to. If I have a son tonight, I will just have to hide him. How, I do not know." Then it was time to stop talking and start working. An hour later she held a beautiful son in her arms.

She smiled with that contented expression that comes over a woman when she first holds her newborn. Pulling back the cloth from his face, she stroked his cheek and little lips. As I packed my things to leave, I thought of the Egyptian soldiers who would delight in flinging this baby to the crocodiles if they knew I'd just delivered him. I shuddered, then looked at Jochebed, who was oblivious to any thought of fear.

"Look how beautiful he is. He is remarkable!...Yes, you are. You are exceedingly fair, my little son," she cooed to her baby. "Oh, Amram, I've never seen a child like this before. Just look at him!"

"Jochebed, he is well formed indeed," the proud father said. He leaned into his wife and cradled the infant's tiny head in his big hand. "Perhaps he will be of special service to God."

"Look at this child, Amram! He is beautiful! Now that I see him I am no longer afraid of the Pharaoh's edict!" Her husband kissed her hair and caressed his son.

"Amram! Let's hide him!"

Look Who Rocked Moses' Cradle

She lived thirty-three centuries ago, just an ordinary Hebrew mother with extraordinary faith. Jochebed's name is mentioned only twice in the Bible; her name is not even given in the Exodus 2 account of Moses' birth and early childhood. We don't know much about her background except that she was born in Egypt to Levi, and was the wife of Amram, as well as the mother of Miriam, Aaron, and Moses. She lived in a very humble home in or near the capital city of Egypt.

To understand Jochebed we must understand her world. First, these were extremely hedonistic times despite the fact that Egypt was a prosperous educational and cultural center. The prominent Egyptian religion worshipped gods represented by animals and included bizarre religious practices. Sadly, many Israelites were enticed into this Egyptian idolatry. Against this backdrop, Jochebed and Amram clung to their faith in God.

Second, the times were especially treacherous for a Hebrew woman. The Israelites had been living in Egypt for 400 years (about 1800–1400 B.C.), but not with the amity enjoyed during the reign of Joseph. Instead, they had become the slaves of the Egyptians and received cruel treatment. Although Egypt had become a vast world power, its leaders had become alarmed at the fruitfulness of the Israelites. Despite the slavery, God's people continued to multiply. Their population had increased to the point that Egypt felt threatened. When oppression didn't reduce their numbers, the Pharaoh tried another approach: murder. He called in the two chief midwives who served the Hebrew women and secretly ordered them to kill all the males they delivered. They gave the necessary lip service to the Pharaoh, but ignored his command and let the babies live. When questioned about their failure to follow through, they just said, "Those Hebrew women are vigorous. They have their babies before we get there." And Pharaoh bought it. God blessed the midwives because they feared God more than Pharaoh.

But when the Pharaoh saw the number of Hebrew males still increasing, he resorted to a more drastic method: If a Hebrew woman had a boy baby he was to be thrown into the Nile! Can you imagine what it must have been like to have been pregnant when that order was decreed? What terror in knowing that if you had a son, he was doomed to die. That is what Jochebed faced.

But Jochebed was a courageous woman who trusted God enough to turn to Him, rather than being immobilized by fear. The Bible tells us three times that Moses was not an ordinary baby (Exodus 2:2; Acts 7:20; Hebrews 11:23). Boldly, Jochebed and her husband decided to hide their baby in violation of the pharaoh's order. You can imagine how every little whimper of her newborn son must have made Jochebed's heart flutter. What if someone heard him and turned her in?

As Moses grew, Jochebed undoubtedly prayed for divine guidance. That is just what she received. When she turned to God, He inspired her thinking and channeled her fear into creativity and action. He gave her the cleverness and wisdom to devise a plan and the courage to carry it out.

Reading this story when I was young, I thought she simply hid the baby, put him in a basket on the river, and lo and behold, the princess found him. Scripture doesn't give us many details, but now that I'm a mother I'm drawn to Jochebed's possible thought process as she devised her plan. Perhaps she remembered that the princess bathed at a particular spot on the Nile. Maybe she knew what time the princess usually arrived. Perhaps Jochebed even knew that she was childless and wanted a baby. I have no proof, but my mother's heart makes me think that she knew these things about the princess before she ever thought of putting her child into the dangerous river.

She wove a basket of papyrus reeds (which they thought was a natural repellent against crocodiles) and covered it with tar and pitch to make it watertight. That reminds me of the little "Moses basket" I used to keep my firstborn cozy. One night my baby would not quit crying. I found nothing wrong when I checked on her, but later I discovered the source of her cries. As she kicked in her basket, the soft lining had fallen down and the basket had cut her tiny feet. I felt terrible! Jochebed, however, was smarter than me. Scholars suggest that she covered the inside of the basket with clay to make it smooth. She was a faithful and ingenious mother.

Well, you know the story. She doubtless went over the plan numerous times with her daughter Miriam. Can't you just picture her final caresses before she put him in his basket? How could she not stroke his hair, cuddle him into her neck as she rocked him, kiss his little cheek and his nose, and smell his sweet breath? As she laid him in the basket did she touch the soft spot on his head and run her finger down his arms, his legs, his toes? Did she have to blink back her tears in order to clearly see his beautiful face one more time before she wrapped him up in the blanket and carried the basket to the edge of the Nile?

She placed the precious basket in the reeds so it wouldn't be swept into the current and had Miriam watch from a safe distance. Here's something else my mother's heart tells me about Jochebed's faith: I'm sure she fought against incredible fear and sadness, but I know she was *assured and convinced* that the princess would find her baby. What mother in her right mind would instruct her daughter to watch if she thought her baby was likely to get eaten by a crocodile or drowned? If she thought these might happen, she certainly would have protected Miriam. A lesser faith might have said, "Miriam, go back to the house. We'll commend him to God, but if something happens I don't want you to see it." But not Jochebed. She was faithful that discovery by the princess would bring her baby to safety. I picture Jochebed sending her off with these words, "Watch carefully; do what we've practiced. You'll do fine…and pray, Miriam, pray!"

She had obviously coached her daughter well. Miriam watched while the princess discovered the basket and sent her attendants for it. Had Jochebed instructed Miriam exactly when to approach the princess? I think so. Exodus 2:6,7 says "She opened it, and saw the child. He was crying, and she felt sorry for him. 'This is one of the Hebrew babies,' she said. Then his sister asked Pharaoh's daughter, 'Shall I go and get one of the Hebrew women to nurse the baby for you?'" Miriam said the right words at just the right moment. Did Jochebed tell her daughter, "Don't go too soon or it will look suspicious. Don't wait too late or she'll leave with him and we'll miss our chance." As soon as Miriam saw compassion in the princess, she was there with exactly the right words. Jochebed had trained her daughter to be obedient and courageous.

What joy for Miriam (and her mother, who was probably also nearby) when the princess answered "go" to Miriam's question. As a mother I wonder how Jochebed was able to play it so cool when her heart had to be pounding. And our babies know us! Did Moses coo or smile too much when she took him from the princess? I also wonder…did the princess figure out the whole thing and play along? But then blessing upon blessing—God allowed Jochebed to nurse her own baby and *get paid for it too!* Don't you know there had to be some joyful lullabies and prayers of thanks as she safely rocked her baby that night?

> *"Jochebed lives on because she walked humbly before her God and because she transmitted character to her son Moses, her daughter Miriam, and her older son, Aaron. She lives on, too, not by how many big tasks she accomplished, but by how wisely and well she served as a mother."*

> —Edith Deen

Her Influence

Jochebed nursed Moses (for a considerably longer period of time than in our culture), then watched over him until he was about three. Some sources say he may have been older. It's also likely that the princess did not completely cut off Jochebed's ties with Moses after that. Moses' heritage was not a secret to anyone. Both he and the Egyptians knew he was a Hebrew. Even though he was the adopted son of the princess, the largest influence in his formative years was his Hebrew mother, who instilled in him a profound faith. She taught him to love God, and to revere their religion and race. He had the best education available at that time, which would have included indoctrination in Egyptian idolatry. But it didn't sway him—he remained faithful to God. As Hebrews, Jochebed and Amram knew the promise God had made to Abraham and his descendants. Moses couldn't have missed this. We don't know how many of his accomplishments Jochebed lived to see, but as Edith Deen says, "We do know she had had the satisfaction of pouring great things into his mind and heart during those most formative years of his life."[2]

Jochebed's Three Fears

Jochebed faced three major fearful events in her life. The first was her pregnancy. Right up to the moment of Moses' birth, she faced more obstacles than options. Although the battle was largely fought in her head, I wonder if this was perhaps her greatest struggle—the internal anguish all mothers share about the welfare of their children. Isn't this the place where Satan wins so many battles with women? Yet, Jochebed and her husband were not afraid. They hid Moses and refused to be afraid of the pharaoh (See Hebrew 11:23).

Her second big fear was at the Nile, a place of intense drama. Before I studied her life, I imagined her practically falling apart with fear and sadness as she put her baby on the water. But now I think she so completely allowed God to transform her fear into creative action that she fully believed that the princess was going to rescue her baby!

The third fear was the final big test of faith. The Bible puts it this way, "When the child grew older, she took him to Pharaoh's daughter and he became her son..." (Exodus 2:10). Within those few words lie the incredible pain of separating from the child you carried and nurtured. She willingly, lovingly, handed her child into the arms of another mother, motivated by intense mother-love and faith in God's plan for her child. What a mother and what an influence!

What I'd Love to Tell Jochebed Over Tea

Dear Jochebed,

You must have lived in the very arms of God to have had the kind of faith you did. As I've become better acquainted with you, I yearn to do the same. We face so many fears as women, but you are the best example I know of facing your fears with faith.

At first I thought you were mainly a woman of trust, and you are—you trusted God completely with your child. You trusted Him enough to say, "I know You know what You're doing God, even if I can't see it." But the Bible tells me in the book of Hebrews that you were a woman of faith with "the assurance of things hoped for, the conviction of things not seen." You believed your newborn son would live, and your faith in God was so strong you were *assured* you could safely hide him and you were *convinced* that even though you couldn't fully foresee the outcome, you could launch him out on the Nile anyway. That is why you went from being an obscure Hebrew woman to being listed in the Faith Hall of Fame (Hebrews 11). You saw something special in your child and chose not to be afraid. And your faith was deeply imparted into all of your children, but especially Moses. In the midst of a crisis your faith held strong and was handed on to your kids. You impacted your family, a nation, and ultimately the world.

When I am afraid for my children, I will try to think of you and remember that the faith you demonstrated wasn't just a feeling or some sort of wishful thinking. It involved your intellect, touched your heart, and enabled you to trust deeply enough to access God's creative solutions.

I wonder if you ever whispered to Moses, "Israel needs a deliverer, my son. This is the fourth generation mentioned in the promise. What does God want from you?" You remind me to encourage my children to look for what God wants to accomplish through them. You inspire me to keep from getting bogged down in my trivial concerns and to make certain that I prepare my children for whatever path God may be calling them to. I can picture you tucking Moses in at night, singing songs of the Lord and telling of His promises. This moves me to make sure we sing more songs of Jesus than we do of Disney, and talk more of His *sure* promises than our well-intentioned ones. Thank you, Jochebed, for teaching me how to face my fears and inspiring me to impart an unwavering faith in God in my quiet moments of mothering. May I always have faith in God's plans for my children.

Sincerely,

Lindsey

SIX

❧

Pioneer Moms

The Mothers of the Settlers

Nineteenth Century

Look Who Rocked the World

WHO: *The men and women who settled the West*

WHAT: *Homesteaders, prospectors, ranchers, missionaries,
and countless others who founded towns, developed trans-
portation and communications, and changed the
West from a frontier to a civilization.*

WHEN: *The heaviest Western migration years: 1841–1866*

WHERE: *From the Mississippi River to the Pacific, extending north
to Canada and south to the Gulf of Mexico.*

Today America's borders extend from coast to coast because brave and adventuresome men and women participated in our country's great westward expansion. Rather than feature one person of great accomplishment and his or her mother, as I have done in the previous chapters, I want to highlight the settlers—men and women who rocked the world by moving to the western part of the United States—and their pioneer mothers—the women who left comfortable lives in the East to cross the prairies in the great western migration.

During the busiest migration years (1841–1866), 350,000 people ventured west from the eastern states, Europe, and Asia. Most traveled along the overland route on the Oregon or Mormon Trails from starting points at the Missouri River. At first the trails were uncrowded; between 1840 and 1848 about 18,000 people ventured into Utah, Oregon, and California. But by 1860, almost 300,000 more had journeyed west, which made for a sea of wagons and increasingly unsanitary trail conditions.

What opened the West? President Thomas Jefferson paved the way in 1803 when the vast Louisiana Territory was purchased from the French. In 1850 the Donation Land Act guaranteed settlers 640 acres in the Oregon territory if they farmed and lived on it for four years. Expansion was further fueled by the discovery of gold in California in 1848 and in Colorado ("Pike's Peak or Bust") in 1857. President Lincoln continued the impetus to "go west, young man" with the Homestead Act of 1862: 160 acres of land were offered to homesteaders who would live on it for five years. Land. Adventure. Freedom. People were drawn west by better economic opportunities and a lifestyle change—the same basic motive that compels us to relocate today.

In 1850 the population of the western states and territories was 179,000. By 1890 it had risen to over 3 million. The westward expansion of our country is a gripping tale, the mosaic of hundreds of thousands of individual stories, usually told by and about men. But it is also the story of women. Women who changed the world by venturing west as pioneers. They also changed the world as moms, passing on the pioneering spirit to their children—the settlers who consequently had what it took to develop and civilize the West.

Pioneer Moms

Courageous Women of Character

———————

"There's not half the virtue in being happy when surrounded by luxuries, as when deprived of them."

—MOLLIE SANFORD, 1857

———————

*Y*ou look lovely," I told Allison.

"I'm an old-timey girl!" she said as she twirled her full calico skirt.

"Well, you would just fit right in with Laura and Mary out on the prairie," I said.

"Do you think I'll be the only old-timey prairie girl at the party?" she asked as she stopped spinning to lace her boots tighter.

"Well, if you're not, you'll certainly be the most exuberant pioneer child there tonight. Most definitely the sweetest," I said, kissing her cheek. "Come here and let Mother tie your bonnet."

I made a big bow under her chin while her two older sisters finished cleaning the kitchen. We had to leave for the church party soon.

"I loaded the dishwasher last. It's your turn," one of them said.

"No, *I* did. You load," responded the other.

"I don't want to load. Especially when it's *your* turn."

"Girls. Who wants to *hand*-wash and dry them?" I asked. Silence. I finished tying Allison's bonnet and turned to the other two.

"You know, I've been reading lately about the pioneers," I continued. "We have so many creature comforts compared to them. What I'm learning is teaching me that I have no right to complain! And neither do you two."

"Mom, we've seen *Little House on the Prairie,* and I still think it's her turn to load."

"Yes we have, and yes it is, but come here first," I said and led them to my study. "I want you to see something." I opened a photo-essay book and flipped through several pages of pictures of Conestoga wagons, sod-houses, and women with young eyes and old skin.

"You would not believe the way these women lived. Most of them had children, too. Do you have any idea how girls your age lived 150 years ago, when their families crossed the plains to go west? I've seen *Little House* too, but there's more to learn about the pioneers and settlers than what we see on TV. Can you picture what it would have been like to have lived in one of these wagons for seven months? Then once they arrived they had to homestead—build their homes and make a living from the ground up. Can you see our family doing that?"

Just Imagine . . .

On the Trail in a Covered Wagon,
Near Denver, Colorado, 1865

Stiff muslin flapped in the wind and the loosened wagon cover tie banged against the buckboard. It beat a rhythm to the slow grinding of the moving wagon wheels, magnified by the vast silence of the plains. Incessant flapping was a small price to pay for the cool breeze my youngest needed on her fevered skin. It was also practical. Who knew when her nausea would hit again.

"Mama, I feel sick," she moaned.

"Well, honey, just lean your head out the back like before. I'll hold you."

"Can Papa please stop?" she asked.

"I wish he could, honey, but he can't. We have to get to our new home before the snow does."

"Are we racing?"

"You bet your bottom dollar. And your Papa's determined to win." I turned to my oldest two girls. "Why don't you two walk for a bit. Give her some room. Just be careful gettin' out." They quickly stepped over their sick sister and scrambled out the back, happy to stretch their legs beside the slow-moving wagons. I took a wet handkerchief and wiped my child's face.

"You'll be just fine, honey. Your tummy's just tired of bein' jostled in this wagon, that's all."

"All of me's tired of it, Mama."

"I know, baby, I know." The children didn't even bother asking how much farther anymore. I pulled her into my lap and tried to get comfortable, but my stiff body felt every board of the wagon bottom through the feather pillows. I snuggled her against me, and in spite of the day's especially rough ride, she fell asleep as I stroked her damp hair. I looked at my little cherub and suddenly found my thoughts drifting back to the parting on my mother's front porch.

Had it really been almost six months since she'd knelt to clutch this child tightly, with tears streaming down her face? I never could stand to see mother cry. I quietly sobbed as each of our four children went to her for their good-bye hug. And I'll never forget the sight of my husband and my father silently shaking hands, then embracing in front of the loaded wagon. I can still see those two stoic men moved beyond words, their dark figures outlined against the billowing white wagon cover. What was it Mother said again? "You are an angel. I'll just close my eyes and see you, dear, until we meet again. Know I'm praying for you every day." There's nothing like a mother's words. Would there ever be another parting as painful as that?

A bump jostled me off my pillow and my mother's porch, back to the reality of the wagon. I laid my slumbering daughter beside me and wiped my nose on the edge of my apron. I figured I had another hour before we stopped, and I would have to haul out the camp stove and send the kids for kindling. If we were lucky. Lately it had been buffalo chips. I dreaded the cooking tonight. It was hard enough when everyone was well to keep the fire stoked sufficiently to cook the biscuits. I wondered how soon I could get an iron cookstove after we built our cabin. I closed my eyes and thought of the lovely curtains I would make when we were finally settled at our new homestead.

"Wake up everyone. A farm!" my husband yelled. I sat up wide-eyed.

Oh, fresh milk. Fresh eggs. Thank You, God.

We approached the homestead and the older children ran ahead. "Oh, look Mother...pumpkins," Claire called back to us. They ran up to the rough-hewn log fence and climbed on the bottom rail for a better view.

A man wearing boots and a homespun brown jacket walked from the barn toward our wagon as we pulled the team to a stop.

"Good day, folks. I'm Floyd McGroom," he said politely as he tipped his straw hat and sidestepped a chicken in his path. "My wife, Opal, is inside. Could we offer you some hospitality?"

"Good day to you, sir. We would be most obliged."

We gratefully tumbled out of the wagon into their welcoming cabin for our first decent meal in ages.

We savored every bite of the hot stew and the yeast bread. Of course, we'd have enjoyed *anything,* as long as it was a change from our beans and salt-pork.

"Ya seen any Indians lately?" Floyd asked Tim.

"No, not a one, actually."

"We heard there was an Indian party on the move. They say they're cuttin' off the wagon trains bringin' supplies. Besides danger, that's bringin' some high prices."

"Well, we'll be on the lookout. Thanks for the warning." They moved their conversation outdoors and all the children followed. Talk of Indians and hide-and-seek with other children was almost as exciting as Christmas.

I grabbed a tea-towel and turned to Opal, a pretty woman in a blue-and-white calico dress with brunette hair peeking out from under her bonnet. "The companionship of women is scarce in this wilderness, isn't it?" she asked as she washed the dishes in a tin bowl.

"Oh, I haven't spoken to another woman in ages. Ever since we separated from our wagon train."

"What happened?"

"It's a long story."

"I've been yearnin' for a long story," Opal said, her eyes dancing. "Tell me."

"Well, we joined the wagon party in Independence like so many, and things were fine at first. Then, one of the men in our party figured he would make a better leader than the one we had. They got testier with each other by the day." I finished the last dish and pulled up a chair in front of the fire, which crackled in the big, open fireplace. A kettle of coffee hung over it by a wire handle. Opal grabbed a hot pad and two tin cups. The aroma of coffee and wood smoke filled the tiny cabin while she poured. I closed my eyes and breathed deeply.

"What'd they do?" she asked, handing me the steaming cup. She sipped her coffee, then reached for her sewing.

"Oh, they made life miserable for us all. Their wives got into it, too, and we all thought there was going to be either a cat fight or a duel. It just about came to that. The troublemaker got so mad after supper one night that he picked up his shotgun in a rage. His little ones started cryin' and his wife just sat there wringin' her hands."

"Then what?"

"Then, just when we thought we were going to have to start diggin' somebody's grave, a Mr. Sanders from another wagon runs up to our fire circle just a shoutin', 'It's her time! Somebody get the midwife! It's her time!' The other ladies and I got the midwife and ran to her wagon, wondering why he was in such a dither. Then, between contractions, his wife told us they'd lost their last baby just eleven months ago."

Opal stopped sewing. "Did this one make it?"

"Yes, but just barely. The baby was already coming when the midwife got there, so it was pretty frantic. The men forgot all about their feud and started playin' their fiddles and harmonicas to keep from hearing Mrs. Sanders."

"Oh, isn't the lack of privacy on the trail just unbearable? I hated that part of coming west," Opal said. She sipped her coffee. "Do go on."

"Well, you could still hear her some, then all of a sudden her wagon got real quiet and I thought Mr. Sanders was goin' to pass out—'til they told him he had a new son. The next morning we waited a few hours longer than normal to start out again. This was just enough time for the train leader and that troublemaker man to get into it again."

"After a night like that?"

"You bet. Only without his shotgun this time. That cantankerous man decided at the next opportunity he and his family were headin' out on their own."

"What was Mrs. Cantankerous doin' this whole time, and did Mrs. Sanders know about any of this?" Opal was clearly enjoying the female conversation.

"Well, she just clammed up, which we were all grateful for, and yes, Mrs. Sanders knew there was trouble, but frankly, I doubt she cared. You should have seen her little babe!"

"Oh…" Opal sighed, "I love babies."

"Me, too. I'm just glad I didn't have to have any in that wagon."

"Amen, sister." She resumed her sewing and asked, "So how'd your family end up on your own?"

"Almost everyone in the Sanders family got sick, so we hung back to help them for a few days, thinking we could eventually catch up with the wagon train. We didn't. Then, when we hit the South Platte River, the Sanders headed north on the Bozeman Trail for Montana, so we've been on our own all the way across the Colorado Territory. I can't tell you how good it is to talk with another woman."

She smiled at me over her sewing and agreed. Two tin lanterns and an oil lamp on the table gave the small room the homiest glow. I was envisioning my own cabin in the not-too-distant future, now that we'd made it this far west.

"I see you've been busy getting your harvest put up," I said, eyeing the strings of drying squash, peppers, onions, and other vegetables that hung from the rafters. A few cheesecloth bags held tiny tomatoes in the final stage of drying. A wooden tray held soap that had been cut into bars and was almost hardened.

"Yes, we're almost ready for winter."

I scanned the rest of the small cabin. An embroidered sampler, a peg rack with an apron, and a crocheted shawl hung on the wall. A small sideboard held some candles and a copy of *McGuffey's Eclectic Reader* and a Bible. A stairwell in the corner led to the sleeping loft upstairs.

"What brought you to the Colorado Territory?" I asked.

"Same thing as most, I imagine. Free land and a chance for a better life. Mr. McGroom couldn't pass up President Lincoln's Homestead Act three years ago. I remember him saying, 'Mrs. McGroom, just listen to this! One hundred sixty acres are yours for the taking if you are willing to work and improve it. Imagine...free land to those who'll homestead it.' So we sold many of our things or exchanged them for the goods we needed to make the crossing...like you folks probably did. We secured a good wagon and team, and bid our relations a painful adieu. Six months later we staked our claim on this parcel of land. It's been hard work, but we've built up a nice little place. The five of us have been happy here."

"Tell me, Opal, what did you find more difficult, the long wagon journey to get here or establishing your homestead?" I asked, thinking of all the hard work that brought this little haven into existence.

"Well, each had its own hardships, but also its own joys." She leaned back in her chair. "I thought we'd never get here, the journey was so long, but there was such freedom then, too. And homesteading is exhausting, but then you look around at what you've built as a family and you realize life is good. God is good." She smiled contentedly, and I suddenly knew why so many of us had left our comfortable life back East.

The men and children came back in, and just before the fiddle music drowned her out, Opal said with a twinkle in her eye, "You know who you have to meet? Mollie Sanford." Then she was up off her chair, picking up the nearest child for a lively dance in the tiny cabin.

Look Who Rocked the Cradles

Pioneer moms rocked the world in two ways. First, they were movers and shakers themselves, leaving behind the creature comforts of their lives in established towns in the East for the unknown of the western wilderness. Second, they rocked the cradles of children who inherited their pioneer spirit, settlers who went on to make homes in the new frontier. Through their stories we can glimpse that pioneering spirit and the legacy they passed on to their children.

To learn more about these women, I read numerous biographies and studied their diaries, personal letters, and family histories. The character qualities these women shared help define who they were and of what they were made. In them we see trust, courage, self sacrifice, faith, and hope.

Trust

One of the most important traits of these women pioneers was their willing spirits. To become pioneers, they first had to be willing to go. That willingness was based on trust in their husbands and in God. Such trust was necessary for them to willingly leave their homes, family, and friends to go west with their adventurous husbands and young children. Can you imagine if all of the wives of these adventure and fortune-seeking men had simply said, "No, I'm not going. You go look for fertile ground or hills of gold alone or with your fevered friends. The children and I will stay here with my parents." The West would probably have remained a frontier. For after a short time of raising a few crops or mining a few bags of gold dust alone, the men would probably have returned east for the comforts of their wives and family. Indeed, many men—and some women—did go alone (for men greatly outnumbered women in the West) and others sent for their families later. But these women who were willing to go were important in settling the wilderness.

In 1922, Mary A. Hodgson described her family's pioneer experience in her journal. Writing in third person, she told of traveling west in a covered wagon as a child. It's clear that Mary's mother, Mrs. McDaniel, did not have to be coerced to go.

> *In the early spring of 1853 a large company of people started from Skylar County Illinois, for the Golden West and among them were E. McDaniel, his wife and five small children. Many people thought the mother unwise in venturing with her children, on so long and perilous a journey to the new country, but the good wife, like many another wife of those days, would not let her husband go without her. She bravely said, "Whatever my husband may have to endure, I willingly share." So she prepared to make the journey with him.*

But the journey was far from easy, and saying good-bye wasn't a "see you next Christmas" parting. For many pioneers it was forever.

> *Large covered wagons drawn by ox teams were to be their homes and carry them to the new land so far away. When all was packed, and the time for parting came, relatives and friends, for miles around, congregated to bid them farewell, realizing that perhaps they would never look upon their faces again.*
>
> *It has been half a century since it occurred. My grandmother took me in her arms, and showered kisses and tears upon my face, for well she knew we were not likely to meet again. My heart saddens now, whenever I think of the grief that parting caused. There is a time though, when all good friends must part, and it was but natural that my father should want to go where there were greater opportunities for gaining wealth.*

Days on the Road, a book by Sarah Raymond Herndon that first appeared as a series of newspaper articles, records details of crossing the plains in 1865 and gives insight into what compelled so many to willingly give up so much to travel across the frontier. For many of these women, it was rooted in their trust in God.

> *May 1.*
>
> *As I sit here in the shade of our prairie-schooner, with this blank book ready to record the events of this our first day on the road, the thought comes to me:*
>
> *"Why are we here? Why have we left home, friends, relatives, associates, and loved ones, who have made so large a part of our lives and added so much to our happiness?"*
>
> *"Echo answers 'Why?'"*
>
> *"The chief aim in life is the pursuit of life, liberty, and happiness." Are we not taking great risks, in thus venturing into the*

wilderness? When devoted men and women leave home, friends and the enjoyments of life to go to some far heathen land, obeying the command: "Go, preach my Gospel, to every creature," we look on and applaud and desire to emulate them. There is something so sublime, so noble in the act that elevates the missionary above the common order of human beings that we are not surprised that they make the sacrifice, and we silently wish that we, too, had been called to do missionary work.

But when people who are comfortably and pleasantly situated pull up stakes and leave all, or nearly all, that makes life worth the living, start on a long, tedious, and perhaps dangerous journey, to seek a home in a strange land among strangers, with no other motive than that of bettering their circumstances, by gaining wealth, and heaping together riches, that perish with the using, it does seem strange that so many people do it.

The motive does not seem to justify the inconvenience, the anxiety, the suspense that must be endured. Yet how would the great West be peopled were it not so? God knows best. It is, without doubt, this spirit of restlessness, and unsatisfied longing, or ambition—if you please—which is implanted in our nature by an all-wise Creator that has peopled the whole earth.

To see God's leading, and trust Him enough to put their feet where their faith was, demonstrates the kind of faith I want to live by and teach my children.

Courage

This is one of the most obvious traits that comes to mind when thinking of the pioneer women. It took amazing courage to brave the wilderness, wild animals, Indians, solitude, storms, deprivation, separations, back-breaking work, and a multitude of other hardships. But nowhere did courage surface more fiercely than when a mother had to defend her children.

Fear for the safety of children can cause women to tap into courage they never knew existed or find it miraculously bestowed. Mrs. Hendee, an early settler's wife, knew about that kind of courage. One day, she was working out in the field while her husband was away on military duty. Indians entered her house and kidnapped her children. They carried them across a river which was a hundred yards wide and nearly too deep to ford. When Mrs. Hendee returned from the field and found out what had happened to her children, she was momentarily grief-stricken. Then instinctively, "like the lioness who has been robbed of her litter she bounded on the trail of her plunderers." She dashed into the river, fighting the current until she was safely across.

With "maternal love dominating every fear, she strode into the Indian camp, regardless of the tomahawks menacingly flourished round her head, [and] boldly demanded the release of her little ones." She pleaded for them until her captors finally relented and gave her back her children. She carried them through the river and sat them down on the bank, but wasn't satisfied with only rescuing her own. She again crossed the river and begged for the release of her neighbor's children, which they also gave her. She returned again and again, until all fifteen children had been released. On her last visit to the camp, the Indians were so amazed at her boldness that one of them declared that "so brave a squaw deserved to be carried across the river." She accepted the offer and was carried to the opposite bank, where she then gathered her little group and returned them to their parents. No doubt, Mrs. Hendee was surprised at her own courage that day.[1]

Self-Sacrifice

The self-sacrifice required of these pioneer moms staggers my imagination. One diary I discovered described what it was like to prepare meals for a family of twelve for six months of covered-wagon living. Can you imagine that? It's nothing for us to hop in the car several times a week to go to the grocery store, make a quick stop for some fast food, or arrive home to find dinner simmering in a crockpot and bread baking in the bread machine. But what would it have been like to cook multiple daily meals for twelve people with only the provisions you could store in a wagon? The answer can be found in the *Emigrants Guide to Oregon and California*, a how-to manual for going west. Most of the book was directed to the men, but it did contain this list of suggested provisions: 200 lb. flour, 150 lb. bacon, 10 lb. coffee, 20 lb. sugar, and 10 lb. salt. Cornmeal and dried beans were usually added, and some (the ones who escaped scurvy) brought dried fruit. Except for rations from the occasional farm or military outpost one might pass or wild game and fish one might catch, that was the diet for half a year. As Helen Carpenter remarks in her diary, "One does like a change and about the only change we have from bread and bacon is to bacon and bread."[2]

While on the trail, cooking was a great challenge. It was done outdoors over an open fire, fueled with dried grass and buffalo chips (dried dung), perhaps with a cookstove, but often in a skillet or heavy pot suspended on poles over a fire. The book *Land of Many Hands* says, "James Clyman, a settler, described one woman in his wagon train who, during a downpour, 'watched and nursed the fire and held an umbrella over the fire and her skillet with the greatest composure for near 2 hours and baked enough bread to give us a very plentiful supper."[3]

Mary Richardson Walker was a woman from Maine who traveled over the Rockies to settle in Oregon and whose greatest desire was to be a missionary. One of her journal entries on the trail shows that though the work was long, sometimes patience wasn't. "May 16, 1838. Rose early, kindled the fire, boiled my clothes, finished my washing before breakfast....Rode in the wagon. Mr. Smith short as pie crust."[4]

The risks were many. Most migrants were young families, so there were lots of children to keep from danger. One in five of the women were pregnant during the crossing, and the frequency of serious illness along the way was staggering. They became exhausted and malnourished as they had few if any doctors and mostly unsanitary conditions. They suffered dysentery, cholera, smallpox, and typhoid. They endured storms, broken wagons, childbirth, fear of Indians, and one of the gravest dangers—river crossings. One source reports that one out of seventeen settlers who left for Oregon never arrived.[5]

After the crossing was made, they faced the daunting task of homesteading, of creating a home from nothing but a patch of ground. Many families lived in their wagons while they built cabins, while others boarded in frontier settlements until they could build their own homes. Families worked as a team, children and parents laboring together to build cabins, chop wood, plow, plant, harvest, manage animals, sew, knit, mend, milk, wash, iron, and bake.

Can you even imagine a life that difficult? Can you imagine a trip as risky as theirs? For many pioneer women, the sacrifices they made were magnified because they had once enjoyed a comfortable life in the East. I am humbled by that kind of self-sacrifice. What if my husband, Tim, were to walk in and say, "Honey, let's move. Let's leave our comfortable life and camp out for seven months in the wilderness to get there. We might die on the way, and it'll be relative wilderness when we arrive. But hey, what a chance to make a buck and get some land!" Hmmm...I don't think so!

Studying how they lived makes me so grateful for the ease of life I enjoy today. I'm thankful that there were women who were willing to make such great sacrifices, some beyond belief, to lay the groundwork of living in the West.

Facing the Dangers Alone

It was not uncommon for a frontier mother to be left alone with her children while her husband went in search of food or supplies, work, or war, like the mother in this story retold from an 1880s account.

After a westward journey in a white-topped wagon, a young mother and her family settled in early spring on an isolated bit of prairie land, near a clump of trees and a creek. They subsisted on fruit and wild game while they prepared the fields for crops. In October, her husband and eldest son had to travel to the nearest settlement for winter supplies. The mother (well along in her pregnancy) stayed with the young children and their dog while the men headed out on a journey that would take several days.

This woman had no neighbors, and other settlers rarely crossed their land. One day an Indian party passed by, informing her that there was a war between two tribes, and her husband was passing right through their land. That night after the Indians had left and she'd put her little ones to bed, she sat by the cabin door and prayed, fighting her intense worry for the safety of her husband and son. For hours she stared into the darkness longing to glimpse her loved ones, while the cold wind blew across the prairie and whistled around her cabin.

Suddenly her tired eyes spotted a strange light to the north. She knew it wasn't lightning because it was steady. It was redder than the Northern Lights, and it wasn't in the east, so it couldn't be the first rays of the morning sun. It grew in intensity to a red glare and suddenly she knew the awful truth. The prairie was on fire!

Fear gripped her as she realized that, all by herself, she would have to face the most destructive and dreaded danger to homesteaders. She looked at her children, who were sweetly sleeping, and then at her faithful dog. She had to save them, but how? She figured she only had about an hour before the flames would reach their tiny cabin because there was nothing but a dry ocean of combustibles all around. She thought about climbing the trees, but knew it would be impossible to climb high enough with the little ones. Her only hope was that the fire would be unable to cross the creek a few miles away. The flames lit up the prairie like noon, and she watched the distant tree tops that bordered the creek until suddenly they too were consumed in the crimson blaze. The creek had been crossed! Terror gripped the young mother's heart.

She awakened her sleeping children and hurriedly dressed them. She encircled them in her arms, kissed them, and tried to described the situation as gently as possible.

"My darlings, dress quickly. We must hurry. There's a fire on the prairie and we must leave our cabin. What's that sweetie?...Yes, let's pray very hard. Hurry now..."

Then, for the first time she missed the dog. She called him, but he did not come. As she scanned the horizon for the dog she saw the long unbroken line of the roaring red blaze and billows of black smoke, as far as her eyes could see, racing towards her, destroying everything in its path. She fell on her knees and poured out her heart to God. "Oh, Lord, please save my babies! Save us from this fire. You are our only hope. My babes are in Your Almighty hand....Please show me what to do!"

As she arose, calmed and strengthened, she heard a bark and turned to the door to see her dog come bounding toward her. He grabbed her dress in his teeth and pulled, then leaped back and barked loudly. He ran off, turning to see if she was following. Instead, the scared but steady mother sat down next to her children awaiting either death or a sudden miracle.

The dog returned and pawed, whined, and barked, trying to get her attention. *What does he want?* Then, in an instant she remembered the one thing that might save them—the thing her dog had just discovered—the plowed field! She scooped up her two youngest in one arm and dragged her son with the other as they raced towards safety.

"Run! Run as hard as you can!" she implored as the fire closed in on them. Coughing in the smoke and feeling the scorching heat of the flames, the young mother and her children ran to the center of the field just as the flames fanned out around the edges of upturned dirt, encircling them in a wall of fire. But the tilled earth stopped the deadly assault, and the little family collapsed to the ground in relief.

"Oh, Father of Mercies. What a deliverance!"

They watched the flames consume their haystack in an instant, then their cabin, more slowly, and finally the southern plains and groves. For hours she cradled her children in her lap, stroking their hair until they drifted into a fretful sleep. With her dog at her feet she watched the blaze slowly lose its fury. Then she too dozed.

When the first light of morning woke her, she blinked, trying to awaken from her nightmare. Then she realized she *was* awake. As far as she could see there was nothing but blackened, charred earth and a low-lying cloud of smoke hovering over the desolate ground. What had once been their home was now only a smoldering mound.

There wasn't another house for forty miles and all their food had been burned. As the day wore on she resorted to digging in the ground for edible roots and nuts with which to partially satisfy her hungry children. Diverted by the strange site of their former home, they began to play around the dying fire in childlike distraction. While they played games she scanned the horizon for a speck of white that would be her husband's wagon. But night fell and still he did not come. She took off part of her clothing to warm her shivering children, gave them the nuts, leaving none for herself, and with a pulsating head, sang and cradled them to sleep. Throughout the long, cold night starving wolves howled in the distance, and she gazed at her little blessings praying, "Oh Father of Mercies, please spare my babies."

The next morning her children, crying with cold, awakened her from her brief nocturnal escape to the sight of the slowly dying fire. The morning sun began to slip away under leaden skies and the wind grew colder. Then, when she thought nothing could get worse, she felt something that would have been a blessing thirty-six hours earlier—rain!

Her mind reeled, her body was stiff, but she forced herself to rise and scrounge once more for something with which to keep her children alive. She gathered the last morsels she could find and fell into a heap, her body wracked with pain. *My hour has come. I am to perish beside the ashes of my home with my little ones around me,* she thought as the rain fell faster.

"My angels…Mama is going to go away, but please don't ever forget me. I love you so much….Samuel, please tell your Papa how much I love him…and Ben, too."

"But, Mama," said the confused, tearful boy, "where will you be when Papa comes?"

The embers hissed in the rain and grew cold as the mother's agony increased by the hour. Then, there beside the ruins of her home, lying prone on the drenched, scorched earth, she gave birth to a child that was spared from ever knowing the pain of that day.

Much later in the day the woman opened her eyes to the horror of her stillborn infant, then she lapsed back into unconsciousness, deaf to the cries of her terror-stricken children. Each time she opened her eyes and tried to stir, she fell back into insensibility. Finally, her oldest boy roused her.

"Mama, I see Papa's wagon!" All day he had been watching the speck on the horizon until he could make out the sight of their wagon. It was slow going as the wagon wheels struggled in the mud. When the father and son saw the black prairie they were terrorized. Finally, within sight of the ruins of their home, they abandoned the wagon and began to shout as they raced the last mile. Reaching his family, he could scarcely believe what he met: starving children, the remains of their home, a dead newborn, and his dying wife.

He took off his coat and put it over her as he gently picked her up into his arms. With tears streaming down his agonized face he looked into her glassy eyes and bent close to her. Slowly, she whispered the terrible story. He wiped the rain from her face softly as he inwardly decried the day he had been lured by the beauty of the prairies, accusing himself of her murder.

"Please forgive me, my love. Please forgive me," he cried softly through his tears.

"There's nothing to forgive," she whispered. "I love you....Don't cry, dear... Pray..." she said with a fading voice. "Father, watch over my...beloved husband and children." Then she closed her eyes the final time.

For two days and nights the distraught husband wept and mourned over his wife, then he laid her remains in the prairie sod near her beloved home which had once shone with her presence.[6]

When I first read this true story I kept waiting for her rescue. Yet along with so many young pioneer women, she paid the ultimate price of self-sacrifice—her life. Her story is not so unusual. A common life-span for pioneer women was about thirty-five years. Yet, despite the high mortality rate and the hard life, the spirit of faith and hope flourished among them.

Faith and Hope

The term *pioneering spirit* has become synonymous with a "can do" attitude in the face of hardship. These strong, tenacious women endured a hard life but were spurred on by the flames of faith and hope. In diary after diary, I read women's accounts of their struggles mixed with the tandem threads of their faith in God and their ever-present hope of brighter things to come.

One Montana mother knew both a hard life and the fuel of faithful hope. She, her husband, and their five children lived in a two room cabin in a mountain gorge thirty miles from any settlement. While he eked gold from the mountain, she raised all the corn and potatoes they needed, did all the housework, and sewed all the family's clothes. Even after surviving sickness and three Indian attacks, her faith and hope never wavered.

When we first came there was no end of bears and wolves, and we could hear them howling all night long. Winter nights the wolves would come and drum on the door with their paws and whine as if they wanted to eat up the children. Husband shot ten and I shot six, and after that we were troubled no more with them.

We have no schools here, as you see, but I have taught my three oldest children to read since we came here, and every Sunday we have family prayers. Husband reads a verse in the Bible, and then I and the children read a verse in turn, till we finish a whole chapter. Then I make the children, all but the baby, repeat a verse over and over till they have it by heart; the Scripture promises do comfort us all, even the littlest one who can only lisp them.

Sometimes on Sunday morning I take all the children to the top of that hill yonder and look at the sun as it comes up over the mountains, and I think of the old folks at home and all our friends in the East. The hardest thing to bear is the solitude. Once, for eighteen months, I never saw the face of a white person except those of my husband and children.

But I am too busy to think much about it daytimes. I must wash, and boil, and bake, or look after the cows which wander off in search of pasture; or go into the valley and hoe the corn and potatoes, or cut the wood; for husband makes his ten or fifteen dollars a day panning out dust up the mountain, and I know that whenever I want him I have only to blow the horn and he will come down to me. So I tend to business here and let him get gold. In five or six years we shall have a nice house farther down and shall want for nothing.[7]

Mollie Sanford

So many of these women have fascinating stories, but my favorite is Mollie Sanford's. I learned of her at the Littleton

Historical Museum, a living history pioneer homestead and turn-of-the-century farm. I located a copy of her published journal and in its pages met someone I liked. Her journal was written on the Nebraska and Colorado frontiers, first as a daughter, then as bride, and later as a mother. I connected with her home and her heart... and history became a bit more real to me through her story.

> *"May the faith that has sustained me through all up to the present be with my children and children's children always."*
>
> —Mollie Sanford, 1895

For starters, we both loved to pour out our thoughts and hearts in our journals, and dreamed of writing books. We both had our first child near our twenty-third birthdays and were both born around our mother's twenty-first birthday. I recently took my children to visit the ruins of a dam destroyed in the famous Cherry Creek Flood. It was an event Mollie had witnessed. After my family and I drove across several states to move to Denver, I echoed her journal entry upon arriving: "The Promised Land is gained and we are in Denver tonight." While we both missed the families we'd left far behind, we loved to "feast our eyes" on the mountains and the country. She and I could each say, "I am content." Here's one thing I especially admire about her: Even when she lived in difficult circumstances—and crossing the plains, homesteading, and a life as a miner's wife certainly qualify—her contentment was not based on circumstances. It was rooted in her faith.

Mollie embodies each of the characteristics we've just discussed. She was trusting (willing to go), courageous, self-sacrificing, and full of faith and hope. Her journal gives great insight into her daily life as she describes traveling across the Plains, the Colorado Gold Rush, and the effects of the Civil War on the frontier. But her writing, often punctuated with a sense of humor, also reveals the heart, mind, and spirit of a pioneer mom.

In 1857, William Dorsey, her father, left Indianapolis for the Nebraska territory with his wife and eight children. Mollie, eighteen at the time, was the eldest and did not have to go. She'd received a marriage proposal, but she refused it to travel with her family. Even as an eighteen-year-old daughter, she was trusting and willing to become a pioneer. While her family was preparing to depart, she wrote:

> I go to a wild unsettled country, where I shall be deprived of all of these; but I go with my dear parents, to share their burdens and their lot, whatsoe'er it be....I have had a pleasant girlhood, but have learned even now that we cannot go through life "on flowery beds of ease."[8]

She also trusted God: "I have faith though that my life's work will be appointed, that my heavenly Father will show me my duties and my way."[9]

Even as an eighteen-year-old pioneering with her family, she showed her optimism:

> Our cabin is of hewn logs, a good-sized room of 20 ft. square, two windows and one door, and a clapboard roof. We are quite settled and look cozy, and if there is not room enough inside there is plenty out of doors, yes! Plenty!!

> Mother hardly enters into extacies (sic). She no doubt realizes what it is to bring a young rising family away from the advantages of the world. To me, it seems a glorious holiday, a freedom from restraint, and I believe it will be a blessing to we girls. We were getting too fond of style, too unhappy not to have the necessary things to carry it out.

> The novelty of this life may wear off in time, but I hope I will have the good sense and judgment to make the very best of our circumstances.[10]

Mollie showed great courage in facing pioneer difficulties such as loneliness and danger. As a bride, she faced the pain of separation when she left her family to cross the plains with Byron, her new husband. "I feel very sad to leave the dear ones. Years may elapse before we meet again, and some of us perhaps never! 'It may be for years, it may be forever,'" she wrote. She endured terrible loneliness. While living in a mining camp and cooking for all the miners, she stole away one Sunday and wrote, "I wished myself a fairy or spirit, that I might fly away to the old home and see them all once more." She wrote a poem reflecting that desire, but she concluded with this spirited response that makes me smile:

> It is pretty hard to come down from the realms of fairies, to the degrading position of cook, but such is my fate, and I suppose these hungry men appreciate my cooking more than they would my verses. I suppose I ought to stick to the one or the other as I cannot make a success of either.[11]

She was also courageous in dangerous situations. I love the way she is able to maintain her great sense of humor.

> We had a scare today. The news was brought in that Indians were on the warpath and would probably attack the mining towns! My cabin stands off alone, so I did not care to stay alone and be butchered. Went to Mrs. Glotfetter's where we could all be slaughtered together. The men gathered all the firearms and congregated in an empty cabin. We had arranged if the worst came to the worst, we would get in the buckets and be let down some of the mining shafts, let down by a windlass, but I said, "No, let me die the death of the brave." I knew if we women were stowed away in the bowels of the earth, and all the men killed, who would rescue us? I would as soon be scalped as buried alive! After a night of suspense, we were informed that it was a hoax. The perpetrator of the joke could not be found or I think there would have been some hair lost, but not by scalping.[12]

Mollie might well have understood one of my mother's exaggerated expressions, "I could have just snatched them baldheaded!"

After her husband decided to try his hand with a mining company, Mollie became the cook for eighteen to twenty men in very primitive accommodations. Her description paints a vivid picture of the self-sacrifice required.

> There is a rough log cabin, neither chinked nor daubed, as they call it, no floor, and only a hole cut out for a door and window. A "bunk" is made in one corner. This is covered with pine boughs, and on this are spread our comforts and blankets. We have no mattress—can't even get straw or hay to fill a bed tick. I have to cook out of doors by a fire, but have mustered my small cook stove into service, but that will only hold one loaf of bread, or one pie at a time. All I have furnished to cook is bread, meat, and coffee. The cups and plates are of tin. A long table is made in a shed made of the pine boughs outside the cabin. No table linen is supplied. I fear I shall sink under this burden. It is not what my fancy painted it.[13]

Days later she describes the continuing difficult sacrificial work in a way that even homemakers today can probably relate to: "The week has been spent in monotonous routine. Cook, cook, bake, bake!" But then she goes on, writing of her difficulties and her delight, "The fire to cook by is built in a pile of rocks. They get so hot that it almost burns my face to a blister.... Called at a cabin and had a sight of a new little baby a week old. I should call her 'Treasure' if she were mine."[14]

In spite of incredible tasks amid harsh conditions, she valued stretching her mind and possessed undaunted optimism.

> I do take a little time now and then, amid all my work, to moralize. I will not put myself down to ceaseless drudgery. I must think and read and do something, so that I shall at least not retrograde. 'Tis a glorious Indian summer day; over the

*mountains and plains hangs a soft hazy mist that gives everything
a calm, subdued effect. Soft breezes are wafted into my cabin
door. I love everything and everybody today. I look upon these
beauteous surroundings and bless the hand that made them.*

In so many of the pioneer writings, examples of faith and
hope are interwoven, as faith is so apt to breed hope in the midst
of abundance or deprivation. Suffering what would be considered poverty by our standards, Mollie expresses thankfulness to
God: "I scour my pine boards, and, looking at the clean smooth
floor, I am admonished that after all I am a little better off than
in 1860, when the bare ground was all the floor I could boast of.
I sing my cheerful songs, and in my heart thank kind Heaven for
my accumulating blessings."[15]

When the Civil War broke out, Byron joined the Colorado
Volunteer Infantry and Mollie became, to her surprise, a soldier's wife. One of their partings (when she was sick) depicts
not only their love, but Mollie's spirit and faith:

*It was not for me, sick and almost helpless, to shrink from the
sacrifice. Other wives had to do the same. Other hearts were as
tender, other loves as fond. I never shall forget the moment
when we came to say good-bye. There were a thousand men
encamped around, all hurry and confusion, and no time nor
place for one word in private....I stood by my husband in the
midst of those men, only wishing for one moment when I could
abandon myself to grief, but I saw the tears trickling down By's
cheek, and then all the heroic in my woman's nature came, and
I turned to be the comforter. I heard a voice saying, "Trust in
Me; I will that ye shall meet again."*

She introduced her "sweet baby boy," Bertie, in her journal,
saying he was born the day Abraham Lincoln issued the Emancipation Proclamation. She called him a marvel of loveliness:

My hands are so full of work, and my head so full of lullabies that I have no heart for poetry, but I meditate when I can. I sit and hold my boy, and dream sweet probabilities for his future, and O! my baby! May you fulfill the fruition of your mother's hopes.[16]

Her next line in that journal entry describes living conditions that we might consider inhumane...and yet she still shows a cheerful attitude.

My fortunes have changed again and now we are living in a tent. We could not get a room. Our winter is delightful and so far we find it very comfortable. It is 12 by 30 feet, two apartments, and I enjoy it....Bertie is called little "Co. H." Born and bred as he has been in the midst of military surroundings, who knows but that he may make a great General![17]

Winter... in a tent... with a baby! And to think I've ever thought I had it bad!

Her greatest hopes were for her children and a lasting legacy:

With my two little ones, I will have less time to journalize. I hope to spend it in caring for them in helpless infancy, training their young minds through childhood, on up through life, should they be spared to me. I pray for grace, patience, and judgment, and for long and useful lives for us all. I shall keep this book as a reminder of the past, and a help for the future.[18]

Mollie Sanford did not want to be forgotten. While not wanting to put herself forward as a heroine, she wrote, "Perchance something I have said or done may be a help to my posterity, for trials and tribulations come to all. May the faith that has sustained me through all up to the present be with my children and children's children always."

What I'd Like to Tell Mollie Over Tea

Dear Mollie,

You and your pioneer sisters were amazing. Before I met you, my knowledge of you pioneer women left me wavering between incomprehension and guilt. I have so much and still sometimes struggle. How did you manage with so little? My curiosity about your lifestyle has turned into respect for your character.

It's difficult to comprehend the extent of your hardships, the lack of privacy, the constant specter of death. Even you were not immune from losing a baby on the frontier. But your experiences were more than the sum of your hardships. I know. You told me in your journal.

You honored and enjoyed the Lord's day as a true Sabbath—a day of rest. Your writings overflowed with your love of the land, nature, newfound freedom, and God. Your journal reflected happy times of singing and music around a campfire, joint sewing, knitting and quilting bees, community barn-raisings, dances, and weddings, and the high point for so many—church.

I am touched by your resourcefulness, your creative spirit, and your love of beauty. Old photographs of white linens under a noon meal by the dusty wagon and stories of adorning a wooden cabin with calico chintz remind me of the joy of simple touches of beauty. The mom who soaked old boots and remade the leather into shoes for her barefoot children, challenges me to be less wasteful and more resourceful in my comfortable world of abundance. The mom who painted a piano keyboard on an old plank and sang the notes while pointing to the "keys," reminds me that we can find many ways to teach our children things that we value with the resources we have.

You didn't have much leisure time for nurturing play or one-on-one with your children, but you impacted them by the life you lived before them. You trained your children in skills and faith. You taught them that a commitment to family was vital to survival. You inspire me to continue that legacy. I wonder—as life has gotten easier and we strive for success, not survival—if perhaps our faith and work ethic as a nation has correspondingly waned.

Mollie, you wrote "perchance something I have said or done may be a help to my posterity, for trials and tribulations come to all." That has happened. I have learned from you as will many others who pick up this book. You have made a difference in the world.

I'll think of you, Mollie. And I'll try to remember to be more thankful and slower to complain. You remind me that to have a legacy, I must be a mom of character. Instead of allowing fear or a lack of security to take root in my relatively secure, abundant life, I'll remember what you've taught me. I will trust my God and my husband as he follows our God. I will choose to be courageous and willing to sacrifice for the good of my family. I will teach my children that faith is the key to survival in this life and necessary for entrance into the one to come. And I will forever hope...not just for a better world, but that my children and children's children will know that faith.

Sincerely,

Lindsey

SEVEN

Helena
The Mother of Constantine
A.D. 255–330

Look Who Rocked the World

WHO: *Constantine*
WHAT: *The first Christian Emperor*
WHEN: *A.D. 274–337. He reigned from 306–337.*
WHERE: *The Roman Empire*

Few people in history can make as strong a claim of being a world changer as Constantine the Great, son of Constantius Chlorus and Helena. His father was the Western coemperor of the Roman Empire, so upon his death Constantine became emperor. However, he wasn't the only one who wanted to rule, and in those turbulent times several men were battling for this position.

One of those battles made Constantine famous and changed the course of Christianity, which was the object of persecution at that time. Just before the battle at the Mulvian Bridge, near Rome in A.D. 312, Constantine and his army saw the image of a cross shining in the sun with the words *In hoc signo vinces*, "In this sign conquer." (Another version of the story says Constantine saw the sign of Chi-Ro, the first letters of Christ, written in fire in the sky.) That night, he dreamed of the sign and became convinced that victory depended upon the power of Christ. The next day, he had crosses inscribed on the shields of his soldiers. Even though Constantine and his army were outnumbered, they won the battle.

Constantine was the first Roman emperor to make Christianity legal. No longer would Christians need to fear retribution for their faith. He also banned the gladiator games, convened an important church council (the Council of Nicea) that ruled against heresy and defined doctrine, and issued many other laws reflecting his Christian sentiments. However, not all historians are convinced about the purity of Constantine's motives. Perhaps, they suggest, he was using Christianity to further his own agenda. Even if that is partially true, Constantine took great risks on behalf of the Christian faith. There is much in his legacy for which we can be thankful.

In 337 Constantine was baptized on his deathbed and then succeeded by his sons. Constantine's personal faith commitment continues to be debated, yet he rocked the world by bringing about a great change in the Roman Empire by allowing Christians to worship freely.

Helena

*A Mom Who Served Where God
Placed Her*

"Helena continues to be revered, for in the seventy-five-year
span of her life she brought to God the homage and tribute
of her devotion."

—EDITH DEEN

They were definitely burned. There they sat:
rock hard, crispy, blackened disks pretending
to be cookies. So, it was going to be one of
those days.

"Mommy, these look like mud pies!" my daughter said, rather
pleased.

"Actually, they're mud bricks. Feel like building something?"
I asked, trying to scrape the cookies off the sheet. "What I need
right now is a chisel...no, maybe a shovel."

"You're really going to build something?" she asked.

"No, I'm just trying to get these off my cookie sheets," I
replied.

"When Daddy shovels, he says to put your weight into it.
Try that."

"Thanks for the advice, Honey. Remind me to write that
down next to this recipe."

I had promised cookies, so by George, we were going to have cookies. I got out all the ingredients...again, found a new recipe, and did a Julia Child number in my kitchen.

Once some chocolate chip confections finally made it to my wire racks, I exchanged my chef's hat for my impression of the Tidy Bowl man. They can put a man on the moon so why can't they invent self-cleaning bathrooms? I muttered as I donned rubber gloves, "Perhaps I should call NASA about this." I picked up Betsy-Wetsy and Rubber Duckie, sprayed the bathtub cleanser, and waited for "thousands of scrubbing bubbles" to do their magic. Of course they needed my help, so I scrubbed along. *They forgot to mention this in the commercial,* I thought.

But as I worked along, I couldn't get the recent meeting of our home fellowship group out of my mind. It had started out like any normal gathering. We shared lots of food and even more laughter. Then, as usual, we turned the topic to spiritual matters. Tonight's discussion was on "doing our part for God." We are all good friends, but as differing opinions were presented by people who held very strong convictions, it began to get a little intense. Not ugly, just impassioned. One man who shared had started a street ministry. He frequently took food and blankets to homeless people living under bridges, then he shared the gospel of Jesus with them. "People are dying out there without Jesus! We are all commanded to go and evangelize!" he stated with strong emotion.

Another friend, who worked in a law firm, shared his view of lifestyle evangelism. "I work with white-collar professionals who need Jesus as much as your street people. I'm trying to make a difference to men who wouldn't listen to a preacher in a pulpit or a witness on the street, but will sometimes listen to a colleague." Different approaches, different ministries.

I left that meeting disturbed. I knew my mothering was eternally valuable, but I felt so left out of their conversation. I felt disconnected from the bigger picture of doing something to make a difference for the kingdom of God. I began to pray for God to show me how He could use me where I was.

Three weeks later I still couldn't get that out of my mind. One friend was saving souls under bridges. Another was impacting the kingdom in the corporate world. Everyone but me was doing something to serve God. I was at home changing diapers and scrubbing tubs in domestic isolation. As I scrubbed I thought, *I'm not really accomplishing anything.* Swish. Swish. *This tub's going to be dirty again in a few days. How can I be used by God here? Folding diapers for Jesus? Scrubbing tubs for the kingdom?* Scrub, scrub. *If God asks me how many souls I've won, I guess I could just tell Him I've been up to my elbows in rubber gloves and rubber duckies.*

Then I stopped worrying and started praying, thanking Him for the opportunity to serve my family. I offered this as service to God—burned cookies and all.

Later that afternoon, a young salesman knocked on my door. Normally very cautious of strangers (and preferring to keep my cash) I usually ignore these intrusions, but today was different. With the safety of my husband's presence inside, I stepped onto the porch and listened to the young man. Somehow, an hour later, without any forethought, I found myself leading him in a prayer to receive Christ. Before he left, my excited seven-year-old (who suddenly saw her mother as the next Billy Graham) brought him cookies (the good ones), and we sent him off with food for the body and spirit.

After he was gone, it suddenly dawned on me what the Lord had done. He had met that man's need for Jesus with my desire to serve. And He did it right on my doorstep. I was so excited I couldn't stand it. Not only because the man found salvation, but because God loved me enough to answer my prayer and bring me an opportunity to serve Him *right where I was!*

Just as he did for Helena. She served God in the quiet life of motherhood and then later from a position of power. Although I can relate to her role as a mother, I cannot help wondering what it must have been like when she became the Empress Mother of the first Christian ruler of the Roman Empire. Later in her life she set out on a trip to help advance Christianity and rediscover the historic and sacred sites from the time of Christ. I wonder what it would have been like to have joined her on her expedition...perhaps attending her highness as her lady-in-waiting.

Just Imagine . . .

Jerusalem, Early in the Fourth Century

Gravel and earth slid under my feet, and I lurched forward to keep from tumbling down into the excavation sight. I had to stay steady because I was steadying the Empress Mother. Slightly behind me, she held my shoulder for support as we slowly made our way down the rocky terrain. I had to be careful; she was nearly eighty years old. All around us workmen were busy digging and hauling dirt and debris.

"We are almost there, my Empress," I said assuringly.

"Well, hasten then. I may be old, but I'm not crippled," retorted the spirited lady with a wink.

I picked up my pace some, but just before we reached level ground she gripped my shoulder.

"Stop. Look at that! Let us take it all in for a moment," she said breathlessly, whether from exertion or emotion I couldn't tell.

The scene before us was staggering to comprehend. We were at the tomb of Jesus.

Silently we looked at the wall of rock and dirt before us and the opening carved out of it. There was a square door with two steps that had been chiseled out of the stone. I helped the Empress Mother sit down on a rock, but her intent eyes never left the doorway. Lost in thought, she wore the paradox of a faint smile and a single tear. I understood. I was simultaneously overcome with sadness at the thought of Jesus' dead, linen-wrapped body placed in that very tomb and the joyful realization that we were sitting somewhere quite near, maybe even on, the very spot where Mary Magdalene first discovered that the stone had been rolled away.

"Can you feel it? Do you feel just a hint of what she must have felt when she saw the open doorway?" Helena whispered. In the sunlight, the blackness of the cave beyond cried out "Empty!" just as Mary Magdalene had found it to be so many years before.

"Just think!" said Helena. "Somewhere, so close to where we are that we might even touch it, is the very spot where Mary thought she saw the gardener outside this new tomb owned by Joseph of Arimathea."

"Only it was our risen Lord Himself!" I added.

"Exactly. Risen on the third day from this very tomb, just as He said." We sat in silence for a moment.

Suddenly, there was a loud crash. I looked above the tomb opening and noticed scores of workers hurrying about. Atop the tomb was a huge mound of dirt. Atop the dirt were the remains of a pagan temple. The demolition was almost complete. Only the right corner wall remained, its carved statue of Venus jutting from the wall in defiance of the holy site below. The queen's workmen had saved this last bit of destruction for her to witness.

"Empress, look! They want you to see the final destruction of this cultic temple," I told her as she stirred from her meditation and looked in the direction I pointed. With three more solid blows, Venus fell and shattered as lifeless as all the Roman cultic idols.

"Ever since I had my workmen begin destroying that temple and excavating for Christ's tomb, I knew it would be found! And now, as my son told Macrius, a beautiful and magnificent church will be built in this place. I will see for myself that the Church of the Holy Sepulchre is constructed," Helena said with conviction.

"Yes, you have traveled a great distance for that very thing," I replied, standing up and helping the empress to her feet. "Do you want to inspect the adjacent site?"

"Of course," she answered, "but first, let's get a closer look here." We stepped over a small culvert. "Look at this ancient irrigation canal they've uncovered. This clearly used to be a garden," she explained. I walked right up to the tomb and ran my hand along the doorway of the smooth, cold cave.

"It's cut out of solid rock. And look!" she exclaimed. "There's a channel carved right in the front. That had to be for rolling the round stone into place to seal it. This is His tomb. It's just as Scripture describes it."

"You are realizing the dream of your pilgrimage," I said. "The workers have been busy doing your bidding. But the bishop wants you to join him on top of this hill as soon as possible. They are unearthing something there this very hour. It's only about 100 meters from here."

"But of course, my dear." The upward ascent made her short of breath, but it wasn't what made her stop in her tracks just before the peak of the hill. Meeting her, the bishop bowed and kissed her hand, then stretched out his hand toward a group of laborers who were slowly lifting a large, wooden cross from the dirt.

She put her hand to her mouth and gasped, her knees buckling slightly. I caught her arm and she leaned on me.

"Is this what I believe it to be? Is it what I have dreamed of finding?" she asked in awe.

The bishop answered reverently. "Yes, Your Highness. It is as you thought. This is the hill of Calvary, and before you is the cross of our Lord."

Helena pulled away from me and slowly, but deliberately, went to the cross and knelt at the foot of the newly excavated holy relic.

"Begging your pardon, Empress Mother," I cautiously ventured, "before us is a cross. We do not know for certain that it is *the* holy cross. Perhaps we should continue to investigate."

She reached out to the cross, running her shaking hand along the splintered wood. Then I knew. Whether this was an ordinary Roman tool of death or the actual holy crucifix we sought, Helena believed it had once held the body of our Lord. She laid her head against the spot where His feet would have been impaled and wept. The tresses of her braids were caught in the splinters, but she didn't notice as she finally pulled away, still overcome.

"I did this," she cried softly.

I knew she did not mean the excavation.

"All of us here. We did this! And everyone before us and after us. Our sins put Him on this cross! His feet were here, bleeding!" She reached up and touched the place. "His hands were there bleeding...for me." She looked up at the crossbar where His arms would have been outstretched, secured with spikes. Locks of gray hair fell into her face as she buried her eyes and cried. I joined her, equally moved at the sight before us.

One of the men supporting the cross asked the bishop what they should do with their burden. He turned to Helena, who heard the question and looked up.

She sniffed and stood up. Wiping her hands on her imperial toga, she declared with renewed strength in her voice, "I will have this sent home to my son. Constantine is rebuilding Byzantium as the new Christian capital of Rome. It is to be called Constantinople. The cross shall go there so that all of Rome, and the world, will see and follow Christ. My pilgrimage has been a success. Now I can face the end of my years in peace, knowing that I have been used by God."

"My Empress," I said quietly, "I must remind you. While God has used you greatly on this journey to help the poor, build churches, and find these amazing holy artifacts and places, I believe that He used you for His purposes long before we traveled this great distance."

"How is that?" she asked quizzically giving me her full attention.

"Before you were an Empress Mother on an important mission, you were a mother influencing a son, who has influenced our world for Christ. That, I dare say, is your greatest accomplishment."

She placed her hand on my shoulder as we turned to descend the hill, then nodded and smiled through her tears.

Look Who Rocked Constantine's Cradle

Helena was one of the earliest pilgrims to the Holy Land, and she has sometimes been called the first Christian archaeologist for her discovery of some of the possible locations associated with Jesus. Her biggest claim to fame is the legend that she found the actual cross on which Jesus was crucified. Most scholars doubt this, but she was canonized as Saint Helena nonetheless. She also found what she believed was Christ's garden tomb, buried underneath a pagan temple that had been erected at that spot. She had the temple destroyed and built the Church of the Holy Sepulchre there.

One writer says this of Helena's legendary discovery of the cross: "With a true flair for the dramatic, the bishop at Jerusalem unearthed a 300-year-old-cross from the earth of Calvary that had mysteriously never seen the ravages of time, soil, and wood-boring insects. While this relic may have been planted in an ingenious plot by the bishop to create an ancient artifact, a holy relic, and a miracle before the eyes of the eighty-year-old empress, let us not allow the intrusion of archaeological facts [to] ruin the impact of a good story."[1] The point is that Helena believed the cross to be genuine. Her discoveries, and the churches she had constructed at some of those sites, have encouraged Christians over the centuries and secured her place in history.

Her personal history, however, is a bit of a mystery. We know she was born in the third century, perhaps around A.D. 255, but historians do not agree where and to whom. Many historians say she was born in Asia Minor as the daughter of a poor innkeeper and that she later worked as a barmaid. They cite as evidence that the emperor Constantine renamed the town of Drepanum in Asia Minor in her honor—Helenopolis, which they say must have been her birthplace.

Others support the tradition that she was born in Britain as the daughter of King Coel of Colchester. You remember him: "Old King Cole was a merry old soul…" Same guy. So, she was either a rags-to-riches ancient cocktail waitress (later converted), or the princess daughter of a Mother Goose star. Either way, that's a pretty colorful start. If she were born a British princess, she would probably have been raised a Christian since Christianity was well established there by that time. Today, many churches, streets, and buildings in Britain are dedicated to her.

> *"Last night in a dream I saw the Cross itself—the very wood which bore the burden of our redemption. I saw how it lay in Jerusalem deep hidden beneath the earth, till the world should be ready to receive it. And a voice said, "Seek and find, and the leaves of the tree shall be for the healing of the nations."*
>
> —*Helena,* from Dorothy Sayers' play
> *The Emperor Constantine*

She became either the mistress or wife (depending on your tavern girl/princess view) of a Roman soldier named Constantius Chlorus and in 274, they had a son—Constantine. Sadly for Helena (and countless others), those ancients weren't a very romantic lot. They didn't place the value on a love-matched marriage that we do; instead, they valued making the right connections. When a better connection came along, in a cold, but culturally acceptable move, Constantius divorced her after nineteen years of marriage so he could marry "the boss' daughter."

To better understand that, and how Constantine rose to power, I'll present a quick overview, but first let me divert briefly. These Roman names can cause one to stumble a bit over the facts. You see, they just changed a letter or two and named everyone in their family practically the same thing. (Helena's husband was Constantius, whose son was Constantine, whose sons were Constantine, Constantius, and Constans, and whose sister was Constantia. Enough already! I'm telling you, these people were *not* very orginal.)

The Roman Empire wasn't in great shape at the time. Those with high political aspirations knew they'd better make sure their wills were in order, for the army would put someone in power, let them reign for a short time, then conveniently slip them a deadly little drink or a turkey leg seasoned with poison in order to make way for their new choice. How anyone in Roman leadership could keep an appetite, I'll never know. Well, Emperor Diocletian (who persecuted Christians) came up with a plan to bring stability to the empire and, hopefully, save his skin. He said, "Hey, let's split the empire into an eastern and western division with two emperors, and for fun let's call ourselves Augusti. Then let's appoint our own successors and call them our caesars. They'll help us rule, then later we can abdicate the throne, they'll step up, and if everyone stays friendly, no one will get killed." (I admit that these were probably not his *exact* words.)

So Rome is ruled by Diocletian in the east and Maximian in the west, with Galerius and Constantius (Helena's husband) under them. They all decided there should be some intermarrying to ensure their safety. Maximian told Constantius, "Hey, I'd love for you to be my successor, but I really need you to marry my daughter." Constantius said, "Consider it done." That meant, of course, that Helena was history.

Now, the augusti and the caesars were busy watching their backs. Galerius didn't want Constantius to try anything funny so he said, "I think I'll take your son to live in my eastern palace.

Besides, my boss Diocletian insists." First Helena lost her husband, then she lost her son. As planned, Diocletian and Maximian abdicated, and Constantius and Galerius moved up, making Constantine's dad an emperor. When Constantius died, Constantine moved up. Before long the whole system fell apart, so a mad scramble for the top started again. Constantine fought for power (with a second Maximian) and eventually became the sole emperor of the Roman Empire. *Voilà*—that's why Helena got divorced, Constantine had to leave, and how he became king-of-the-hill in Rome. Sounds like a mini-series, doesn't it?

After all those years, Constantine had not forgotten his mother. One of his first official acts was to send for her, and restore her to her rightful place of respect as the mother of the emperor. He distinguished her with the title of Nobilissima Femina—Most Honored and Noble Lady.

Her son didn't just elevate her as a ceremonial gesture. He truly respected and honored her as his mother. He also knew she'd been through a lot. Her status had gone from serving as a mother to being robbed of her family and suffering political exile. But after a lengthy time in that sad, lonely phase of her life, she was elevated to the position of Empress Mother. Helena could have become a cold-hearted, bitter woman over that abandonment, but she didn't. Bitter people aren't particularly effective, so instead of remaining mired in the pain of her past, she made the most of wherever she was. And God used her.

Helena used her influence with her son to counsel and advise him. She went from being a political outcast to a woman with a powerful unofficial position—she was able to bend the ear of the emperor. Like so many other women who've recognized the God-given gift of female influence, she became the woman behind the man, a gentle force behind the throne.

Helena was a devout Christian and greatly influenced the attitude of her son toward Christianity at a time when Christians were thrown to the lions and paganism was the primary religion. We don't know precisely when she became a believer. If she was the innkeeper's daughter as some historians say she was, her conversion may have come about the same time as Constantine's. These scholars who hold to her British origins say she had been raised as a Christian, therefore she had presented her faith to her son since his birth, at the same time that other children of noble descent were being raised as pagans. Either way, Helena encouraged her son to accept and promote the Christian faith. Her greatest service to posterity came from this role; her son was the first emperor to declare Christianity a legal religion.

She wasn't just a cheerleading mom in the wings, however. In her role as mother of the emperor, she used the power and the privilege befitting that title to embark on a journey to spread the Christian faith when she was nearly eighty-years-old—a job she undertook with zeal! She courageously set out for Palestine and the eastern provinces, not an easy task when you consider the difficulty of travel in those days. This was the journey that made her famous, although that was not her intent. In Palestine she was searching for the original historical sites connected with the life, death, and resurrection of Jesus. At many of these places she oversaw the building of churches. One was the Church of the Nativity (at Bethlehem) built over what many believe was the original location of Jesus' manger.

Were the locations she discovered historically accurate? That point has been much debated. In 1885, British General Charles Gordon discovered what he believed to be Golgotha, and it perfectly matched the description in the Bible. But we may never know for certain which is the actual spot of the crucifixion. Still, for centuries, Christians have made pilgrimages to the churches Helena founded. And although many other buildings have been added to the Church of the Holy Sepulchre over the centuries, the original building that she had constructed more than sixteen centuries ago *still* exists.

Besides building churches on her journey, Helena showed that she was a woman of compassion by helping the poor, especially the poor in the Holy Land. Edith Deen writes, "The poor were special objects of her charity. The ecclesiastical historian Sozomen says that 'during her residence at Jerusalem, Helena assembled virgins at a feast, ministered to them at supper, presented them with food, poured water on their hands and performed other similar services customary to those who wait upon guests.'"[2] It is no surprise that she was lovingly greeted everywhere she went.

When Helena died in A.D. 330, Constantine honored her with a ceremonious burial and ordered coins minted in her name, along with the initials of the title he had bestowed upon her.

Helena was a woman who used her power, privileges, and position to make a difference in the cause of Christianity. Whether in her home or in a palace, Helena served passionately where God had placed her.

What I'd Love to Tell Helena Over Tea

Dear Helena,

On the surface it seems that there is little in common between my life as an ordinary mom at the turn of the twenty-first century, and your life as mother of an emperor in the fourth century. Practically speaking, this is true. But I see some connecting threads between your story and mine.

First, I respect the way you used your power and position *as a mother.* Even when you served in anonymity, you had a strong impact because, as mothers, we are women of *influence.* You raised your son to be a man of character, and championed his Christian causes. Had that been your only service, it would have been a mighty, world-changing one. It reminds me that I should pour myself wholeheartedly into my job of being a mother. You are an example to me of the fact that when, with joy and zeal, I allow God to use me in this ordinary place He brings forth fruit from my efforts in the lives of my children. When I'm on the homefront rather than the forefront, God can use me mightily. I can raise my children to know and love God, bring soup to a sick neighbor, or pray with a troubled friend.

The second common thread we share is that God sometimes uses us to serve Him from positions of leadership. Women serve as company presidents, association chairpersons, ministry leaders, and leaders of thought and culture. We can make a difference. You allowed God to use you for His service when He placed you in a strategic position later in your life. I respect the way you used your position to further the gospel of Christ. Helena, at that time in your life when you could have relaxed and enjoyed the plush life of the palace, you undertook a long, difficult mission trip because of the passion God placed in your heart to make a difference in the world. Your example inspires me to look beyond my comfort for ways to further the kingdom and do my part in fulfilling the great commission—to go and tell others of Jesus' sacrifice on the cross and victory over death at the tomb...for us all.

You remind me that God uses me in big ways in the small things of life. Thank you, Helena, for reminding me to open my eyes to the ways God can use me *where I am.*

Sincerely,

Lindsey

~

EIGHT

Catherine Carmichael

The Mother of
Amy Carmichael

d. 1913

Look Who Rocked the World

WHO: *Amy Carmichael*
WHAT: *Pioneering missionary to India, poet, author, hymnwriter*
WHEN: *1867–1951*
WHERE: *Born Millisle, Northern Ireland; served in Japan, China, Ceylon, and India.*

Amy Carmichael's story is one that has touched many hearts and changed many lives, for at the heart of her amazing work in India we find a soul uncommonly abandoned to God. Amy, the oldest of David and Catherine Carmichael's seven children, was a high-spirited child who developed great compassion for hurting people and those in "utter darkness" who did not know the love of Christ. She knew at an early age that God had plans for her.

As a teenager, Amy hosted neighborhood children in her home (with her mother's approval), taught a night-school for boys once a week ending with a "good-night service," worked at the YWCA, and founded a group of Christian young people who committed themselves to reading the Bible and praying daily. She also started Christian meetings for the "Shawlies," poor mill girls who, not owning proper Victorian hats, covered their heads with shawls. The meetings outgrew the church hall and eventually had to be moved to a building that could seat 500.

Amy's desire to serve was made difficult by poor health, which occasionally forced her to rest for weeks at a time. The first mission board to which she applied refused her because of her health. In spite of this, a year after she heard the call she left for foreign soil, serving for fifteen months in Japan, then China and Ceylon, and finally India. Ignoring the objections of Indian Christians and missionaries, she wore an Indian sari and stained her exposed skin with coffee so she could minister more freely. Her life's work was the Dohnavur Fellowship, a home for children rescued from the abuse of Hindu temple worship. Many of these children had been brought to the temple as infants and committed to a lifetime of being "married to the gods" and being available to male "worshipers."

When Amy left her home for India, it was for good. For fifty-three years she never left her adopted country, not even for a vacation. But her mother was able to come to the Dohnevur Fellowship for a time. In 1931 Amy had prayed, "Do anything, Lord, that would fit me to serve Thee and help my beloveds." That same afternoon she had a crippling accident that left her a semi-invalid, often in pain for the last twenty years of her life. It was during this period that she wrote many of her thirty-nine books, mulitplying her ministry far beyond the borders of her adopted country.

Amy Carmichael exemplified selfless discipleship, obedience at all costs, and a bold faith. Although she remained single, Amy was a "mom" who changed the world—during her lifetime almost 1000 children were rescued, educated, trained, nurtured, and introduced to love from God, through Amy. They called her Amma—mother. The ministry she founded is still in existence today.

Catherine Carmichael

A Mom Who Trained Them
Up to Let Them Go

"There never was such a mother—so good, so loving, so
unselfish, so perfect in every way, we can only thank God for
her and try to make her shadowed life bright with our love."

—AMY CARMICHAEL

---

hey almost sparkled. My children wore their
Christmas best and excited expressions of expectation as they waited for our approval on their
performance in the Christmas program.

"How was it?"

"Yeah, what'd ya think?"

"Mommy, did we do good?" they all said at once.

"Daddy and I loved it," I answered. "More importantly, I know
Jesus loved it! I saw you all singing to Him."

"I guess you guys wouldn't want ice cream, would you?" Tim
deadpanned. The three young players and their older sister
thought that was a fabulous idea, so we headed for the Golden
Arches across the street to celebrate.

At the restaurant we got our treats and sat down, with the
children excitedly chattering between bites. Then out of the
corner of my eye I saw him. The tray of half a dozen small hamburgers first caught my eye. The rest of him was not hard to

miss, even in peripheral vision. He was dirty. His hair and beard were scraggly. His pants were ripped and ragged, and he wore several layers of worn shirts. I didn't notice a coat, though it was snowing outside. And when he ate, it was with the ravenous appetite of a man who hasn't eaten in a while. *Oh, Lord, this man is in need*, I silently prayed.

Soon my children noticed him, and their chatter quieted as they finished their dessert. They looked at us with big eyes and we responded with a look that said, "Think before you speak. We'll talk about this outside." When the last drop of ice cream was scraped from the cups, we made our way to the car. I couldn't help noticing how their pretty holiday clothes contrasted with this man's rags. I winced at the glaring disparity.

We'd barely gotten outside when they all four began to talk at once.

"Did you see that man?"

"Why was he dressed like that?"

"Why'd he have so many little hamburgers?"

"You guys, we've *got* to do something to help him! We *can't* just leave!" The six of us stood silently thinking for a few seconds in the parking lot.

Claire began to fumble in her backpack purse. "I have two dollars," she said. Jacquelyn joined her. "I have five. Mom, Dad, how much do you have?" We all examined our pockets and purses and pooled our meager fist-full of dollars.

"Well, it's not much, but it's all we've got," I said. "Who wants to take it to him?" Jacquelyn volunteered to be background support if Claire would be the designated spokesgirl. We waited, observing through the windows. In a moment they had finished their mission, left the restaurant, and raced toward us.

"You should have seen his face!" they said.

"What did you say, Claire?" Tim asked.

"I held the money out," Claire bubbled, "and said, 'My family wants you to have this. And we want you to know that Jesus loves you. Merry Christmas.' Then he took the money and said 'Thank you,' very quietly."

"Oh, you guys, isn't there anything else we can do for him? When Claire gave him the money, he had a tear in his eye," Jacquelyn said. She did, too.

The ride home became a child-led brainstorming session about the homeless and what we could do to help. Each one of them brought their own particular viewpoint and ideas to the conversation, and I thanked God for their uniqueness. *How is God going to use each of them?* While they excitedly planned, I realized we had just experienced an incredible answer to prayer. Just two days ago, I had prayed for the Lord to show me how we could help someone this holiday season and begin to teach our children about ministering to others amid the abundance of Christmas. Before I could inquire into ministry opportunities or even give it much thought, God brought the opportunity to us. Then I remembered that Amy Carmichael had said that "opportunities no strategy or plan could have created are most freely and wonderfully given. Our only responsibility is not to miss them as they pass." What if we hadn't been paying attention?

I came to realize there is so much more I can do to give my children opportunities to stretch beyond their own comfortable lives, reach out to hurting people, and develop a compassion for introducing others to Jesus. I wondered what might happen if I prepared myself to let God use them as He sees fit, not as I do. This was the legacy of Amy Carmichael's mother. She knew how to train her children, but then she also knew how to let them walk where God directed, even when it was difficult for her as a mother. What might it have been like if I had joined her in one of those trying places...perhaps as a coworker from her rescue mission, on our way to visit her daughter.

Just Imagine . . .

The Slums of Manchester, England, 1889

A cold, wet mist stung our faces and seemed to seep into our bones as we made our way down the crowded cobblestone street. I pulled my hat down and drew my wool cape tighter. Catherine Carmichael walked next to me, the very picture of a proper Victorian mother—roundish face, but not too round, appropriate necklace and earrings, and, of course, just the right hat. But the substance of Catherine was much deeper than what one could see outwardly. We hurried along, going as fast as her canister of hot soup would allow. We wanted to visit her daughter and return home before these inner-city streets were bathed in total darkness and danger.

"Look out!" I called, grabbing Catherine's cloak and steering her away as a pile of falling garbage thudded to the ground next to us. We looked up to see who was raining trash upon us, and saw a poor, ill-kept girl. She stared at us with somber, lifeless eyes for a moment, then simply closed the window.

"'Scuse me, dames," an unshaven, scruffy man muttered as he bumped into us. We nodded and continued walking, leaving his alcoholic stench behind us. We hurried on.

"Catherine," I said, "I don't like this."

"Nor do I. Let's hurry." She paused a moment. "You know, Amy was mobbed by a bunch of hooligans last week while she was walking to the railway station."

"Oh goodness. Was she hurt?"

"No, a kind lady saw the incident and came out of her house to help."

"Was Amy terrified?"

"No, can you believe it? She just continued on. I tell you, that girl has been different since birth! Fearless and full of adventure ever since she was knee-high."

"It's a good thing," I said as my heart fluttered. "But how does your daughter live on such a street?"

"You see that?" she said pointing to a smoke-stack in the distance that was billowing out black smoke. I nodded. "Well, Amy sees that and it calls out to her. In every puff of smoke she sees need, need, need. This industrial town is overflowing with poor girls working in the factories. She lives here because they live here. She's trying to start a work similar to what she started for the Shawlies in Ireland."

"She's helping your friend Jacob MacGill, isn't she?"

"Yes. Her 'Uncle' Jacob, as she says. He's been kind enough to extend the invitation for us both to work here. He recognized we had a difficult time in Belfast last year when our savings ran out. I never thought I'd be the superintendent for women in a rescue mission, but I am grateful for the work. Besides," she said, stepping over a broken liquor bottle, "the work is fulfilling when the need is so great. You obviously understand what I mean, otherwise you wouldn't be volunteering at the mission with me."

"I wish I could help out more often. My children are still small, you know," I said.

"Yes, we appreciate any help at all," she replied. "Well, here we are. This is where she lives." We entered the dilapidated building and made our way up a worn flight of stairs to Amy's apartment. At the top of the landing, we heard a couple engaged in a verbal brawl behind their closed door. A baby was screaming to be heard over their raised voices. Catherine and I exchanged concerned glances as we passed their apartment and knocked on the next door. In a moment, a drawn, pale young woman answered the door.

"Oh, Motherie! I'm so glad to see you," Amy said, falling into her mother's hug. "Please come in, both of you." She ushered us into the tiny, dingy apartment. Amy laid back down on the sofa while her mother went straight to the tiny kitchen at the other end of the room and took down a soup bowl.

"Catherine?" I asked. "Why don't I make her some tea?"

"Perfect," she replied, pointing to the kettle. I set to work.

"Still up to your old tricks, Mother?"

"What's that?" she said, setting a tray on Amy's lap containing as much love as nourishment.

"You always made hot soup for the sick. Except now I can't be the deliverer like when I was a child. I must be the recipient. I must say that I like it much better the other way." Amy chuckled, then coughed. Catherine tenderly stroked her grown daughter's hair.

"So do I, my dear. You always liked delivering it to our poor villagers more than any of your brothers or sisters. And now just look at you. You are in need. Amy, child, what are we going to do with you?"

"I guess I must rest, but you know how I hate being ill, Mother! There's so much work to be done."

"Darling, tell me again what the doctor said."

"It's something that is affecting my nerves. He said my poor diet, weak body, and the overwork have taken a toll on me, so I must consider changing my lifestyle. I need to get complete rest if I'm ever to regain my health. Oh, Motherie," she sniffed. "My body seems to get in the way of my ministry."

"Now, Amy. If you do not take care of the only body that God gave you, how can you use it to serve Him? Will you use it all up right now?"

"Of course not. I just don't want to give up my work with these factory girls. I feel like I haven't even begun."

"Eeeeh!" I screamed, nearly dropping the cup as a huge, hairy bug crawled out of it. I caught my breath "I'm so sorry. It startled me."

"You have to get used to crawlies around here," Amy responded. "I've cleaned as best I can, but they've infested the building. The most loathly sort of 'puchies' crawl through the thin walls, but my main battle is to keep them out of my food," Amy said, her nose wrinkling in protest.

"They are so nasty," said Catherine. Then, turning to Amy, she asked, "Do you remember what you said of this place when you first came here?"

"Yes, I said it was exactly the sort of place I should have chosen if I had been asked to choose!" she replied with spirit. In the kitchen, I cleaned the teacup and marveled at her determination to serve God despite her present condition. Amazing, considering the comfort she had enjoyed as a child in Ireland. While I cleaned her little kitchen and finished a tea tray, mother and daughter talked.

"You must know," said Catherine, "I am so concerned for you. *Really*, Amy. You push yourself so and live in such a dangerous place. Dear, I beg of you to do whatever it takes to get better."

"Mother, do you remember last year when we first found out that all of Father's savings had been lost in the crash?"

"Of course."

"Remember your reaction? Some of my friends' mothers would have become so distraught and overwhelmed. But not you. Remember? You gathered all of us around you and..."

"We prayed together as a family," Catherine said softly.

"Yes. I'll never forget how we all knelt and committed the entire situation to God. Do you remember what you said?" Amy asked.

"A great many things, I'm sure. What?"

"You said, 'He has been so kind about other things that we cannot doubt but that He will care for this, too.'"

"Mmmm, yes. And God has."

"Mother. He will care for *me* too," she said softly, but intently.

"I don't doubt that for a second, Darling," Catherine replied. I carried the tea tray into the living room and thought, *Yes, but sometimes it is more difficult to trust His care when it concerns your child.* I wondered how Catherine could stand to let her daughter live and work in these conditions. I tried to imagine my little ones, safely home now, growing up to live in slums like this as they served God.

I poured the tea and the three of us visited until leaving could be put off no longer. To avoid going home in the dark, we said our good-byes, Catherine kissed her daughter, and we closed the door behind us. We stepped from her filthy building into the cold, evening air, growing thick with fog.

"Catherine, are you worried for her?" I asked.

"I would be if I didn't know that Amy has an angel guard protecting her!" she replied. "You know, this job requires so much." I knew she was not talking about our work at the mission. "Her father and I tried to train our children to care about hurting people and to love God with all their hearts. I know there was a reason that God made Amy adventurous and full of spirit. Believe me, her mischief-making gave me lots of gray hair when she was little, but now I see that God put that into her for His purposes. The hard part is doing what I know He continues to ask of me."

"Which is?" I asked, imagining her pain for her daughter.

"To let her go," she sighed. I looked down at the cobblestones as we walked and tried to imagine doing this with my wee ones. "Somehow," she continued, "I sense that God has great need of Amy. My job is to release her to Him, no matter how much it hurts." She held her head high and her eyes glistened as we walked home in the fog...away from Amy.

Look Who Rocked Amy's Cradle

Catherine Jane Carmichael rocked seven cradles as a mother. The first one was Amy's. In telling Catherine's story, I shall also be telling Amy's, for they are both "moms" who changed the world— Catherine through her mothering and Amy as a surrogate mother to so many Indian children. Both stories greatly touch me.

Catherine helped change the world because she was a mother who trained up her children well and then she let them go. Let's look at how she did that.

She Trained Her Up in a Happy Home

The Carmichael household was a haven of peace. Amy's early years were spent in the idyllic seaside village of Millisle,

Northern Ireland where she played with her brothers, sisters, and cousins amid rocky beaches, the ocean, and the beautiful Irish countryside. They enjoyed an affluent lifestyle with a comfortable home, lots of books, toys, pets, even ponies. But in spite of this abundance, they were far from spoiled. Catherine and her husband, David, taught their children from infancy to share their possessions and avoid class distinctions.

Catherine was a loving, nurturing mother who blessed her children with lots of lap-time stories and the soothing security of a mother's songs. She balanced her soft side, however, with consistent discipline. Her children knew what was expected, as well as the consequences of anything less. Amy, being a high-spirited, mischievous child, quickly became well-acquainted with these consequences. Her pranks included walking along the gutters of the roof with her two little brothers and later enjoying a sea-spray drenching dressed in her fancy clothes. After being told that laburnum tree seeds were poisonous, Amy said, "Let's count how many we can eat before we die!"

Fortunately, her mother was as consistent in her discipline as she was in her rocking. She required her children to accept their punishment calmly, with a "Thank you, Mother" afterward. Catherine was determined to train her children to handle life's difficulties with grace, as seen in this exchange: When Amy exclaimed, "Oh, Mother, I've such a pain!" Her mother calmly replied, "Have you, Dear? I hope it will do you good." "But Mother, I can't bear it! It's a *dreadful pain.*" "Is it, Dear? I'm afraid you will have to bear it." Now *that* mother was no pushover! This kind of training, combined with Amy's adventurous and fearless spirit, served her well on the mission field when she faced grave difficulties.

Her childhood was serene with "its discipline balanced by buttered toast and raspberry jam in front of the nursery fire."[1] Raised around an abundance of joy and love, Amy said they "got endless fun out of life,"[2] and "I don't think there could have been a happier child than I was."[3] This upbringing gave Amy a strong emotional base, a heart for providing as much happiness as she could, and the kind of love that later permeated the Dohnavur Fellowship.

She Trained Her Up in the Knowledge of God

Amy learned about God through Bible stories on her mother's lap and in daily family prayer sessions, when her father would read scriptures aloud from the King James Bible. And she learned about prayer. Catherine impressed its importance upon her daughter. "Ask God, Amy, if you want anything badly. Share it with Him. He's never too far away to hear our prayers and He'll always give you an answer."[4]

So Amy took her mother at her word. At three years old, she wanted one thing—blue eyes like her mother—and decided to take this request straight to God. She knelt and asked Him to change her big brown eyes to baby blue, quite assured that He would do so. When she awoke, she pushed a chair up to the chest of drawers, climbed up, and looked confidently in the mirror. Her eyes remained brown. She was bewildered at first, but learned a lesson that stayed with her for the rest of her life: "No" can also be an answer. Her mother's instruction was true. God always heard and always answered; sometimes it was "yes," sometimes "wait," and sometimes "no." This was invaluable knowledge, for prayer became the mainstay of her life; upon it she founded and carried forth her ministry. She didn't ask people for money to support her mission work. She only asked God. Little did Catherine realize when she gave this little lesson on prayer that it would be the weapon her daughter would wield to fight intense spiritual warfare in rescuing children from the demonic influences found in Hindu temples.

She Trained Her Up with a Heart for God

In Victorian times church attendance, and even family Bible reading, was common. Many did these things just because it was the proper thing to do. They knew how to look religious. However, both of Amy's parents had a deep love for God and an intimate personal faith in Jesus Christ. They passed this devotion on to their children. For the Carmichael family, church was the highlight of their week.

From her earliest days, Amy was raised to know that God loved her and that He was very real. The reality of a personal relationship with God shaped her life and pointed the way for her future. About one of her earliest childhood memories, she writes, "After the nursery light had been turned low and I was quite alone, I used to smooth a little place on the sheet and say aloud, but softly, to our Father, 'Please come and sit with me.' And that baby custom left something which recurs and is with me still...."[5] Isn't that a beautiful thought? God is so real that we can say to Him, "Please come and sit with me." Sometimes a simple phrase can impact your life, as these six words have mine. I want to teach my children that God is so close, so loving, so very real, that He will indeed *come and sit with us*. But that's not just a message for my children. It's for me. And you. Sometimes when I'm lonely or afraid or in need of comfort, I think of Amy's words...and comfort comes. He comes.

She Trained Her Up to See and Meet the Needs of Others

Catherine Carmichael was charitable and compassionate and gave her children every opportunity to develop these gifts as well. Both of Amy's parents wanted their children to see the needs of others and then act to meet them. When Catherine made soup for the sick or the poor in their village, she sent her young children to deliver it, sometimes before they had eaten their own portion. Kathleen White writes that like Florence Nightingale and others, the Carmichael children "learned to care first by small acts of kindness locally to the aged and infirm."[6]

Catherine modeled compassion by her example. She taught singing and cooking to some of the village girls and made hospitality a way of life. The Carmichael home was always open to anyone who needed the nourishment of good food and encouraging words. When Amy gathered local children for a meeting in her home, Catherine didn't object. Instead, she made tea for them. Imagine the different message that Amy would have received if her mother had replied, "Now, dear, we can't have all those children in this house. I'm too busy." Instead, her actions said, "Let the children come. I'll put on the kettle."

Seeing love in action not only taught compassion, but had an added benefit. In their hospitable, open home, guests were welcomed and some of them had a powerful influence on Amy. Their pastor, John Beatty, was a family friend who played chess with her father, so she got to know him as more than a man who stood behind the pulpit. Beatty's brother also visited, telling the children stories about missionary life in India, which especially interested Amy. Another frequent guest in their home was a woman who told stories of martyrs and taught them to recite poetry. Amy grew to know that real people share the gospel; that India was a needy, beckoning place; and that poetry is beautiful. These influences can be seen in Amy's life. This open-home policy reminds me that the people I invite into my home can plant seeds in my children that may later bear fruit.

She Trained Her Up with Unwavering Faith

When things go well, it can be easy to train and model the qualities we want to see in our children. But when the storms blow, we discover the depth of our roots. When Amy was about eighteen, money became a problem in the Carmichael home because a man who had borrowed money from her father was unable to pay it back. Not long after that, her father became ill and died. Amy became a great help to her mother in dealing with the younger children, forging an even closer relationship with her.

In the midst of the despair that gripped her after her husband's death, Catherine found solace and strength in her faith, particularly in the truth of Nahum 1:7: "The LORD is good, a refuge in times of trouble. He cares for those who trust in him." Amy later discovered her mother had written next to that verse, "Found true all along the line ever since." [7]

When Amy was twenty, a financial crash ate into the rest of their money, but Catherine did not despair. Instead of panicking, she calmly gathered her brood, told them the situation, and knelt with them in prayer. God met their needs during that crisis. The following year, after some of Amy's siblings left home, Catherine, Amy, and one of her sisters left Belfast to work in Manchester, England at the invitation of a family friend.

She Trained Her Up to Let Her Go

She trained them well. She loved them dearly. But mostly, she held them loosely. The thing that inspires me most about Catherine Carmichael was her open-hand hold on her children.

The first occasion in which she had to practice releasing her child was while Amy still lived at home. Her family had relocated to the city of Belfast when she was in her teens. Although Catherine and David loved to surround their children with beauty and shield them from ugliness, she allowed Amy to venture out of her sheltered world into the Belfast slums to minister. Amy joined her friend, Eleanor Montgomery (who taught the boys night class with her) and Eleanor's father, who was with the Belfast City Mission, as they visited the city's darkest streets. Catherine also raised more than a few eyebrows in her straight-laced world when she allowed Amy, as an older teenager, to enter the slums and invite the "Shawlies" to her meeting at church. While others considered this improper, Amy commented, "Perhaps my mother believed in an angel guard."

Amy's mom had her next opportunity to release her daughter when a close family friend, Robert Wilson, whom they called the D.O.M. (Dear Old Man), invited Amy to live with him and his sons as his surrogate daughter. Amy was in her early twenties and Wilson's own daughter had died when she was Amy's age. His wife had been dead some time as well. Although Catherine

was so close to her firstborn and still needed Amy's help, yet in
a sacrificial act of love she allowed her to go live with their dear
friend. For three years, God used Catherine's sacrifice to provide Wilson with a daughter's love, to provide Amy with a
fatherly love, and to receive some spiritual mentoring from this
godly man who would prepare her for what lie ahead.

But Catherine's greatest act of mother-love was that which
cost her the most: She had to completely release her child to
God. It started with Amy's call on a snowy January 13, 1892,
when Amy heard God's voice again. Unmistakably and repeatedly, she heard God clearly saying, "Go ye." With much prayer
and soul-searching, Amy grappled with the practical obstacles in
her way, and finally concluded that God wanted her on the foreign mission field. She tried to explain all of this in a letter to
her mother written over two days. She penned, "My Precious
Mother, Have you given your child unreservedly to the Lord for
whatever He wills?...O may He strengthen you to say YES to
Him if He asks something which costs." She described how God
had called her saying, "Go ye—to those dying in the dark—
50,000 of them every day, while we at home live in the midst of
blazing light." With great difficulty she listed the practical objections to her going: Her mother still had a great need for her, so
did the Dear Old Man, and her health was not strong. "Mother,"
she wrote, "I feel as if I had been stabbing someone I loved...
and through all the keen sharp pain which has come since
Wednesday, the certainty that it was His voice I heard has never
wavered; though all my heart has shrunk from what it means,
though I seem torn in two, and just feel one big ache all over, yet
the certainty is there—He said to me 'Go,' and I answered, 'yes,
Lord.' "

Amy also quoted the words of Jesus that had pierced her
heart: "If anyone would come after me, he must deny himself
and take up his cross and follow me. For whoever wants to save
his life will lose it, but whoever loses his life for me will find it"
(Matthew 16:24,25).

When a child (grown or otherwise) lays their dreams, hopes, and convictions before their mother, they yearn for the blessing of approval and support. A young child who hands her mother a crayon masterpiece wants to hear her mother exclaim, "This is lovely! God has gifted you." Amy must have felt that anticipation as she waited for her mother's response. This was Catherine's reply on January 16 which began with a poem:

> *My own Precious Child,*
> > *He who hath led will lead*
> > > *All through the wilderness,*
> > *He who hath fed will surely feed...*
> > *He who hath heard thy cry*
> > > *Will never close His ear,*
> > *He who hath marked thy faintest sigh*
> > > *Will not forget thy tear.*
> > *He loveth always, faileth never,*
> > *So rest on Him today—forever.*

> *Yes, dearest Amy, He has lent you to me all these years. He only knows what a strength, comfort and joy you have been to me. In sorrow He made you my staff and solace, in loneliness my more than child companion, and in my gladness my bright and merry-hearted sympathizer. So, darling, when He asks you now to go away from within my reach, can I say nay? No, no, Amy, He is yours—you are His—to take you where He pleases and to use you as He pleases. I can trust you to Him and I do....All day He has helped me, and my heart unfailingly says, Go ye."*

Her long, sweet letter went on, expressing more, "of the sufficient grace she could count on, of the everlasting love, of the smallness of life, of her willingness to give her child into the loving arms of God. As for Mr. Wilson, 'God has his happiness in His keeping.'"[8] Mr. Wilson unselfishly wrote to Mrs. Carmichael to comfort *her*. He said, "I know something of what it must cost you, but am sure He who calls for this, will more than fill the void caused, by His own love flowing in....She has been and is more than I can tell you to me, but not too sweet or too loving to present to Him who gave Himself for us."[9]

Catherine Carmichael could have reacted a number of ways to Amy's news. She could have expressed shock, reluctance, fear, uncertainty, or selfishness. She could have been critical, causing Amy to doubt God's calling. She could have given shaky support, such as, "Well, if you think you should, but have you considered..." She could have even objected completely. Amy might have become a missionary even if her mother had responded like that, but can you imagine the pain, the doubt, and the difficulty she would have faced without her mother's blessing? Instead, Catherine gifted Amy with a parental blessing. She *wholeheartedly* and *unreservedly* released her child to God. And the beautiful, loving letter she wrote to her daughter expressing that release freed Amy to follow God's calling. Catherine Carmichael was a mother who trained up Amy in the way she should go...and then lovingly *let* her go...into God's service. And the world was changed.

What I'd Love to Tell Catherine Over Tea

Dear Catherine,

Countless little children in India will always be grateful to you for the impact you had on Amy. She changed their lives. Countless souls have been won for the Lord, as who knows how many young people have joined her in mission work, inspired by her writings and example to deny their own comfort and follow Christ. I wonder what would have happened if you hadn't trained Amy to believe that God hears and answers prayer, that the Bible is true, and that her temperament was a gift from God. What would have happened if you hadn't modeled for her the importance of seeing others' needs and then meeting them. And your example showing that a totally devoted heart for God is the only way to live, even when some around us are content with an easy and shallow faith. I wonder what would have happened if you hadn't been willing to give Amy back to God with your blessing? The world is a better place because of your willingness to train up your child and then let her go.

Your story inspires me to look at each of my children as an individual, each uniquely created by God to be who He made them to be for a purpose. His purpose. While I try to train them in godly and obedient character, I am learning to thank God for the unique bent that He instills in each one. Who knows. What I see as a negative, God may just see as a positive, something He can use in their future. Thank you, Catherine, for waking me up to the fact that I must give my children the eyes to see with compassion and look for opportunities to meet the needs of others. But mostly, I thank you for being an example of our need to return our children back to God. My mother's heart wants to hold them tightly, but I know God wants me to loosen my grip and give them back into His waiting arms.

They want to risk; I want them safe. They want to go; I want them to stay. When I am confronted with fears and doubts for my children as they grow and test their wings, you inspire me to help them fly instead. I pray that as they stretch their wings and leave my nest for the unknown, or soar far away, I will echo your words about my child and God: "He is yours—you are His—to take you where He pleases and to use you as He pleases. I can trust you to Him and I do...." Thank you, Catherine, for reminding me that the safest place for my children is where God wants them.

Sincerely,

Lindsey

NINE

Mom Frey

A Modern Mother

1906–1998

Mom Frey

A Woman of Deeds, Not Words

"She was not a star. She was truly a moon. She reflected the glory of her husband, her children, grandchildren, great grandchildren, and friends, but mostly, she reflected the glory of our Lord Jesus Christ."

The day was pleasant and a bit humid, typical for November in Tomball, a friendly little Texas town near Houston. I drove down FM 2920 with the window down and some country-and-western singer crooning a sad song about lost love. I rolled up the window and clicked off the radio. *No doubt the next song will be about a freight train or a pickup truck.* My thoughts turned to a recent conversation with my friend Lynette.

"I have a theory," she philosophized. "I think if you get good parenting, you're ten years ahead of the game. At least."

"How so?" I asked.

"Well, you don't have to spend time unloading mental baggage, unwinding the tapes in your head, and learning what you weren't taught, like I did."

"It *is* different if you've had someone model proper relationships," I agreed, thinking of my own family and the blessing they were to me. "What about your family?" I asked tentatively.

"I came from a good home. I mean, I know my parents have always had my best interests at heart. They've always been there for me. But the older I've become, the more I realize there were some things my parents didn't do very well. In some ways I think I've grown up 'relationally challenged,'" she said.

"Oh?" I asked, smiling.

"It's so different if you've had someone model what it looks like to encourage one another, how to process pain and disagreement, how to be transparent and share deeply from your heart, and how to welcome people into your heart and home. If you want to grow in that direction, you're ten years behind if you didn't see that lived out in your family."

"Well, ten years behind is tough, but it's better than continuing the cycle. When did you recognize you wanted to be the one to change the legacy?" I asked.

"First in my relationship with my husband, who is good at those things. But also through an older friend who has been helping me, and a lot of other women, reduce the learning curve on our ten years. Things like being an encourager, sharing feelings, being vulnerable."

"Sounds like a family I know from college. They are so good at those things."

I was about to meet Mom Frey, the head of their clan. I'd heard she was 91 and sharp as a tack. I pulled into the drive and walked up the pansy-lined front walk of her immaculate, one-story, red-brick home. The inside was as lovely as the outside. The teal entry, artwork, cherry furniture, and fresh flowers all said, "Come on in. We love company." Even the library, with its floor to ceiling volumes on the dark shelves and its overstuffed chairs made me feel welcome. It was only the long Formica counter and the uniforms that gave away the real identity of the lovely retirement home.

"Betty Frey," declared the brass nameplate on the cherry door of her efficiency apartment. Shirley and Shirley-Ann, Mom Frey's "daughters-in-love" as they call themselves, greeted me with smiling faces.

"Please come in. We're so glad you're here. Mom's almost ready. Why don't you have a seat by the window?"

I put my bag down and settled in an antique chair that flanked a camel-back sofa positioned diagonally in the room. I wondered if that was a statement of style or a deliberate attempt to catch the light. Perhaps it was a just necessity since there was only room for the most treasured of ninety-one years worth of belongings.

I'd been in other retirement homes before, but this place—this woman—was different. At ninety-one a person should have the pleasure of wearing a housedress and slippers if one so desired, but not Mom Frey. I looked up to see a smiling woman slowly emerging from her bedroom. She was the picture of careful grooming in black dress slacks, a white silk blouse, and perfectly coifed white hair.

"It's so nice to meet you," she said in a clear, precise voice.

And so began my visit with this charming woman who changed her corner of the world with deeds of love. Through her stories, I wished I could go back in time and enjoy the simple joys of an ordinary day in the life of this delightful homemaker who had a passion for Jesus and for her family.

Just Imagine . . .

Mom Frey's Kitchen, California, 1943

"Just pull up a chair and sit down. Can I get you a glass of iced tea?" asked my friend and hostess.

"That sounds good, if I'm not keeping you from something," I replied. "I really just came by to drop off these papers. I don't know how I got home with them."

"Oh, I hadn't even missed them yet. I must have put them on top of your Bible at the meeting this afternoon. Thank you so much for bringing them to me." She smiled warmly and took the manila envelope, placing it on her neat kitchen counter.

"Well, it was on my way home. The kids are with their dad at a ballgame tonight, so I had some extra time."

I loved being in Betty's inviting kitchen. It was such a homey place. But maybe it was just Betty. She was pretty, with her soft curls, slim figure, and quiet ways. I always seemed to relax a notch or two when I was with her. She handed me a pretty blue tea glass with a sprig of mint floating on the top, which sure beat instant tea in a jelly jar.

"Oh, good. Then why don't you stay for dinner? I'll treat you to some leftovers," she said, not really waiting for my answer.

"Now, Betty, I don't want to trouble you…"

"It's not a bit of trouble." She was already busy pulling things out of the refrigerator. I looked at the odd assortment of food that began to line her counter. A single leftover baked potato, a large carrot, some green onions, and a boiled egg. What in the world was she going to do with that? She pulled out half a head of lettuce and something wrapped in foil.

"Oh, we're in luck," she exclaimed brightly, opening the foil to find a piece of broiled chicken from a previous meal. One of my motivations in staying was just to see what meal could possibly come from this.

"Well, thanks, Betty. That'd be nice. What can I do to help?"

"Why don't you start cutting up these vegetables while I make the mayonnaise." I grabbed a paring knife, and she began to whip some oil, a raw egg, and lemon juice with her hand mixer. Before I could graduate from the carrot to the onions, she had a small bowl of fluffy white mayonnaise. Betty was clearly in her domain.

We chopped and chatted about our earlier missionary committee meeting at church. Everyone on the committee was a longtime friend of Betty's. Along with our regular business, we had to make sure that Betty knew her husband had volunteered them to host a missionary family the following week. We all remembered the previous summer when he had graciously opened their home to the children of another missionary family—for the entire summer! She'd wondered at the time if he realized what he'd done, but then she entertained those kids all summer by teaching them to cook and sew. She also hosted cookouts. She always was one to "go with the flow" so graciously, like she'd planned it that way in the first place. This time she was well aware of her upcoming guests and looked forward to extending her hospitality. I couldn't help noticing as Betty joined me in the chopping that while I produced hunks of vegetable, she diced.

"What can we have for dessert?" she wondered, peering back into the fridge.

"I saw you had some applesauce. How about that?"

"Oh, no color."

"What?" I asked quizzically.

"Too much white. You know, the potato...the egg...applesauce would be another white. The color has to be as pleasing as the taste. Oh, here we go," and she reached for a jar of homemade poppy-seed dressing and the fruit bowl. "It's not as good as mincemeat pie, but it will do."

"Betty, where did you learn to cook like this?"

"On-the-job training. In my late teens I earned money for college by cooking for a doctor and a wealthy socialite. I didn't know much about cooking then, but I figured I could read a book, so why not a recipe? I learned." The phone rang, interrupting her from her precision slicing. She wiped her hands on her yellow apron and crossed the kitchen to answer it. "Look at those dark clouds, would you?" she said, glancing out the window as she picked up the receiver.

"Hello...yes, this is she." I walked to the back door, opened it, and saw an unusual sight for Southern California. Overcast skies and rain headed our way.

Her brow was furrowed as she twisted the phone cord. "Well, I know they'll be disappointed, but we're not surprised...

Yes…gasoline and tires are in short supply for many people these days. Thank you for calling." She cradled the phone with a look of deep disappointment on her face. "Jack is just going to be crushed," she said sadly.

"What's wrong?"

"The Soap Box Derby nationals have been cancelled. He and Dick have really gotten into these races with their dad, and this year Jack won for our region and was on his way to the national competition in Akron, Ohio. Unfortunately, the official on the phone just told me they've been cancelled this year due to the war. Poor Jack. I'll have to tell him when he and Dick get home from their friend's house. He and his dad have worked so hard."

She finished the dinner preparations while I set the table. "Oh, be sure to use this for Ernie's place." She handed me a fork that was different from the others. "He likes this thick one with four prongs," she said, as she walked out her back door into the yard. Sure enough, the others had three. Attention to detail for those she loved was a hallmark of Betty Frey. She returned moments later with a bundle of greenery and some wild roses, which she quickly arranged in a simple vase and placed in the center of the table. Then she called her husband and young daughter to dinner.

The dining-room table was set on this ordinary Tuesday night with placemats, cloth napkins, and a simple centerpiece. In less than thirty minutes, a couple of vegetables and a few leftovers had been transformed into a delicious-looking salad on a bed of torn lettuce. A dessert plate held a beautiful fruit salad with poppy-seed dressing and toasted sunflower seeds, all on a single lettuce leaf. A basket of Betty's famous whole grain, homemade bread sat near Ernie's place for him to serve, as was his custom. I looked at the colorful, appetizing meal before me and marveled at Betty's impromptu way of taking simple things and making them special. Betty's daughter came in.

"All we're waiting for is Ernie," Betty said. Just then he walked in and took his seat. Everyone stared. I didn't know whether to laugh or not. There he sat, quietly in his place, wearing a sport coat with upturned collar, a top coat, and his hat.

"I take it, Dad, that you're just a bit nippy," she said with a knowing grin.

"You might say that." Even when they disagreed about the temperature of their home, it was done with love and humor. We cracked up. Cold-natured Ernie smiled, removed his hat, and blessed the meal. Then as rain began to pelt the windows, we feasted on gourmet leftovers.

At the end of the meal my friend got another call.

"It's Darlene's baby," she informed me. "She's got a bad case of croup and has had pneumonia before. We have to pray." Then by her living room sofa, we knelt and prayed for God to protect our friend's child.

Before I left that evening, just before dusk gave way to darkness, thirteen-year-old Dick and ten-year-old Jack came in from their friend's house. With four-year-old Julia at her skirt, she greeted her boys at the door with a hug. Betty marveled at the wet world outside in a place where it seldom rained.

Her eyes sparkled. "Come on kids! Let's get on our bathing suits. We're going to play in the rain!"

Look Who Rocked the World

Most of the other moms in this book have been mothers of the famous. Mom Frey raised no one famous. At least not yet. The other moms I've written about have raised offspring with outstanding, highly renowned accomplishments. None of Mom Frey's descendants will be recognizable by name or deeds to the man on the street in Topeka. At least not now. So how can I say they rocked the world? Well, some of us are called to rock the world at large, but others, indeed most, are called to make a difference where we are, in our little corner of it.

Betty and her husband, Ernie, produced a clan of 53 and counting: four children (Dick, Jack, Julia, and Bill), their spouses, 14 grandchildren and 11 spouses, and 20 great-grandchildren.

Those ranks include a preacher, a doctor, business executives, a company president, and several generations of property developers (making the Frey name well-known in Tomball). One is pursuing a doctorate in hopes·of becoming a college president, and another is a missionary in Ethiopia, walking in the family footsteps (Ernie had spent part of his childhood in Africa with his missionary parents). And to the delight of Mom Frey, the clan also includes many dedicated homemakers, a calling she held in high esteem and to which she dedicated her life.

However, those influenced by Betty Frey don't just include those bearing the Frey family name. Because their home was always open to missionaries, her children's friends, church youth groups, and anyone else in need of some nurturing, her circle of influence can be counted as one counts the ripples in a pond—ever widening, growing, continuing to expand.

Now Look Who Rocked Their Cradles

She was called Mom, Grandmother, G.G. (for great-grandmother), Betty to her close friends, and to many others, simply Mom Frey. She was the kind of woman who served up large helpings of good food and unconditional love. Both were plentiful for anybody who happened by her kitchen. She was a college English teacher with impeccable grammar and good diction. She was respected for her knowledge of cooking, sewing, and the Bible. She was an avid gardener and sewed all of her own clothes, even making her daughter's wedding dress. She was also a bit ahead of her time, finding other ways to cook food than burying it in fat and frying. She ordered 100-pound sacks of whole grains from a mill and ground them herself, and she walked every evening with her husband.

Betty prayed faithfully for her family her entire life and found creative ways to teach her children about God. She held sewing and cooking classes for her children, their friends, her grandchildren, and their friends—boys and girls alike. She also charged a small fee for the privilege of taking her classes. "They know that we pay for things of value, and I wanted them to know that these skills are of value," she said.

She was intimately involved in her children's lives from her days as a new mother through her days as a great-grandmother. In my visit with this dear woman she told me, "I have to have some kind of report from my grandchildren. For instance, I asked Ernie, 'What's your goal for this year? What are you doing the next three months? What's your verse for the year, Ernie?'" She remained connected with those she loved.

She was the kind of woman who'd call one of her daughters-in-law, whom she knew wouldn't get to her mending, and say, "Honey, we're going to mend together today." Betty Frey was a woman for whom love was a verb and it meant deeds, not just words.

For Betty, learning was not just something you did in school. It was a lifelong process. She learned to surfboard behind a boat at age fifty-two and *then* learned how to swim five years later. She went snow skiing and ice-skating at sixty-two, rode an ostrich in Africa at sixty-seven, and took piano lessons for the first time at age sixty, which she continued until she was ninety. And she wasn't content with simply learning to play the piano— she took theory as well to keep her mind sharp! Her attitude was: life's an adventure; if I have breath, I can learn!

She was born Elizabeth Julia Hershey, the last of 11 children, in 1906 on an Abilene, Kansas farm. Her father wrote her name in the margins of the family Bible because the lines were already filled. She was so small at birth that the doctor didn't expect her to live, and when her mother took her out, people would ask, "Oh, Mrs. Hershey, isn't the baby well?" Her mother would simply reply, "Oh, she's fine. She just hasn't started to grow yet."

Her family protected her from the difficult outdoor chores of farm life in the early 1900s, but they couldn't seem to protect her from herself, so feisty was her spirit. When her sister, Lois, came down with diptheria, little Elizabeth took note of all the attention and came up with the plan to hide under her father's desk until her mother and the doctor had left. Then she quickly snuck into Lois' room and planted a big kiss square on her sister's lips. Her mission was successful. She soon discovered, however, that the limelight of diptheria proved much worse than the shadow of her sister's illness.

After she was married, both Betty and her husband taught at a college in Pennsylvania, then moved to California during the depression (without their furniture). When baby Dick was born, this excited young mother was enamored with her new baby.

I thought he was the most wonderful baby in the world. I felt just like the Madonna as I would stroll in the afternoons with him in his wonderful little reed buggy. I couldn't understand why everyone was just going about their business and didn't realize what a wonderful specimen I had.

When her son was just a year old she helped care for her sister's twins who were the same age. "That was my chief occupation," she said. "Three little children to feed, diaper, train, and my days were consumed with that." Her husband's coworkers were so intrigued that some of them made an appointment to come by at lunch to watch her simultaneously feed three babies.

With money scarce then, she made lots of sponge cakes from the dozens of eggs she got from her sister's farm, ate New Zealand wild spinach that grew in the yard, and made do with what little she had. In our age today, where the propensity for debt is high and the threshold of contentment is low, Betty's example is inspiring. She said of those frugal years, "We were happy. We *really* were happy."

She believed in the importance of keeping her children occupied. Their home had fruit trees and plenty of space for gardening, so she involved them in that pastime. "I was telling my niece about all the things the boys were doing and she said, 'Aunt Betty, you keep the boys pretty busy.' And I said, 'Yes, I know. They're going to be busy in something. I'm going to see that they're busy in the right things.'" She made them work, but as her daughter Julia said, "She had us bamboozled! She was so much fun, we didn't know if we were working or playing."

Through fun, Betty taught important values about work. Like the cream-puff principle. When Julia was sixteen she made a batch of meat-filled cream puffs to serve for dinner, but unfortunately they were a total flop. Literally. Flopped, flat as a pancake. Only harder. Frustrated, Julia threw them away.

"Tell me exactly what you did," her mother said, so Julia told her.

"But *how* did you add the eggs?" her mom continued.

"I just stirred," said Julia.

"Well, Honey, there's your problem. As the only leavening, they have to be *beaten* in. Let's start over."

"But, Mom, we don't have time," her surprised daughter said.

"Honey, we're making time, so you won't ever be afraid to tackle this again." They did. This time Julia made cream puffs to perfection.

"She raised the art of homemaking to the level of a CEO."

Years later, when Julia had her own family, she took her cooking skills to an inner-city community center and taught cooking classes and principles of nutrition to women. They then shared the food they made with the day-care children there.

But Julia learned far more from her mother's lessons than cooking methods. She learned not to be afraid of failing. When Julia's daughter was struggling to make her own dress for Easter, she cut out the dress with two left front pieces. That certainly wouldn't work. Since her daughter didn't have any more fabric to cut out the right piece, and it was the Tuesday before Easter, Julia told her they'd just go buy a dress. Then she suddenly remembered the cream-puff principle and stopped in her tracks.

"No, we're not. We're going to the store, but not for a dress. We're buying more fabric so you can do it again. I don't ever want the fear of failure to keep you from trying again." And so the principle was passed on to the next generation.

Many people have stories about the wonderful influence of Betty Frey in their lives. Her sacrificial and unconditional love touched countless people. When she was forty-eight years old, she got a call from her son on her birthday.

"Mom? You want another boy?"

"No, I do not. I still have one here," she said. With three children out of the nest and Bill a teenager (born when she was thirty-nine), life was just about to get easier for her. But her son wouldn't take no for an answer. Then he added something that overcame any reluctance she felt.

"Mom, if you don't take him, he's going to waste!"

Three weeks later an illiterate twelve-year-old boy, with a ragged little suitcase and a rough start in life, came to live with the Freys. He stayed for four years. She knew he was embarrassed that he couldn't read, so without letting him know that she was running interference, she went to his Sunday school teachers and asked them not to call on Larry to read in public. Then she told her new charge, "Larry, you have to know how to read. Therefore, we're going to read every day." And they did. Today, Larry and his family recognize how the sacrificial deeds of this woman changed his life—and theirs.

He kept in touch with the family for over thirty years and had this read at her memorial:

> I'm the guy who by coming in contact with Mom and Dad Frey was saved at an early age. I couldn't ever put into words what all I feel in my heart for Mom Frey. She showed me what real love—God's love—is all about. She took a young boy whose life was headed for destruction and turned him into a productive and appreciative man who has joy in his heart that was only put there because of the lifestyle that was lived in front of him daily....How do you possibly thank a person for all that?

There were others who felt like family at the Freys. Like Ty, who raided the fridge after school with Jack. Betty said, "He felt like anything at our house was his. I can just see him flying in on Sunday morning saying, 'Oh, Mrs. Frey, I need a shirt.' We would all be in the car ready to leave for church and I'd say, 'Well, you know where they are. Just go on in and get a shirt.' Which he would do."

Or Keith, who lived across the street. "What impacted me at that age was how much food was always around and how much they loved to cook!" he recalls. She was famous for her bread, now called Frey Bread by many, and Keith loved it. In Betty's later years, when he stopped by with his wife for a visit, she made him a loaf. "Isn't that amazing? Eighty-nine years old and almost blind, but she remembered how much I loved her bread as a kid."

Another high-school neighbor boy hung out at the Frey house often enough to get a haircut by Mrs. Frey on a regular basis. He loved her bread, too, and hoarded it when she sent him some years later in Vietnam. "The legacy of Mrs. Frey," he said, "is that there was enough love in that lady for all the members of the family down through the generations and for folks like me who just happened to be near."

Through her letter-writing and phone calls she stayed in touch with every one of her family, all the way down to her great-grandchildren. Her only daughter, Julia, said, "Whether our interest was cooking, or camping, or football, or fishing, or music, she was always there to help or to watch or to cheer." They say she knew how to play "20 Questions" quite well. "She'd get right up next to you," her grandson Ernie said. "She'd put her hand on your knee and say, 'Tell me.' Pat. Pat. Pat. 'Tell me about any girls in your life.' And her ears would perk up. 'Tell me about the plans you have.' And in the course of a few minutes, you connected with Grandma and made it on her prayer list."

Donald Tabb, one of Jack's college roommates, said, "I would not have come to Christ, served with the Billy Graham team for eleven years, and been a pastor for twenty-five years without the influence of Betty Frey." She also mentored her "daughters-in-love," and they in turn mentored others who continued the widening circle and even influenced me.

Every now and then, if you're really blessed, you run into a person or a family that makes you sit up and take notice. That's what happened the day I visited Mom Frey. I understood why so many people through the years wanted to hang out in her kitchen. She had a way of nourishing you with her presence. She was also fun. At ninety-one years old she was in the middle of planning a cruise with her daughter, Julia. I said, "Mom Frey, I can't believe you're going on a cruise! Are you excited?" She smiled and said, "Oh, yes. It's a great excuse to get some new clothes!"

She later told Julia about our visit and said, "She wanted to know how I had influenced all of you."

"Well, what'd you tell her?"

Mom Frey simply replied, "I told her I didn't know."

But she did. She had shared stories with me of ordinary moments that changed her corner of the world.

She wasn't able to keep her date with Julia. Two months after my visit with her, she went home to be with Jesus. Even at the end of her journey, she was still focused on others. She asked her family, "Is there anyone you know of that I've offended and need to make things right before I die?" They assured her she'd covered her bases.

Her memorial service was more than a eulogy; it was a celebration of her legacy. To a full house of people touched by Betty Frey, her oldest son shared a handwritten note she'd written in the last six months of her life. He said:

> She never had very good penmanship—her handwriting was just horrible. And then when she got blind it was

really bad. But she wrote these things that were important
to her:

- The ability to stand alone.
- The ability to not compromise.
- No limitations on anything.
- Communicate.
- Know your child and cultivate their attributes while
  working on their weaknesses.
- Know that your children are watching you.
- Model the Christian life.

He also shared how on Christmas day, the day after her heart
attack, she said, "Dick, I want to leave a legacy...I want to leave
a legacy." She did. As a college freshman she'd written a paper
titled, "Deeds, Not Words," and that is how she lived her life.
How did she influence others? By showing love in life's simple,
ordinary moments. As she told me, "A lot of things can be com-
municated by how you live."

What I'd Love to Tell Betty Over Tea

Dear Mom Frey,

It was such a privilege to have met you. Through your
family, the personal history tapes you recorded of your life,
some of the women you mentored, and our visit, I discovered
a woman worthy of emulation. You remind me of the impact
we can have in the simple, ordinary work of motherhood.

I admire your forgiving spirit such as when your husband
stopped to fill up the car with gas while on vacation and realized sixty miles down the road that he'd left you there.
Somehow you managed to laugh and go on vacation with him
anyway!

I loved the blessing you gave each of your children and
grandchildren at the end of the tape you made for the family.
As you mentioned your children one by one and stated how

they were special to you, you were moved to tears, weren't you, over each and every child? And then, as you named a character quality you saw in each of your grandchildren and great-grandchildren, you demonstrated your intimacy with them and blessed them just as the Old Testament patriarchs had issued blessings before their deaths. What a beautiful legacy.

Someone at your memorial service was overheard saying, "When I die, I want to have a service just like that." But services like that aren't simply planned. They are earned. Thank you for inspiring me to live my life so focused on passionately loving my God and my family with deeds, not just words, that a "legacy celebration" can be a possibility. I wonder if you've been treated to a glimpse through some celestial window of the numbers of people touched by your life?

In relative obscurity (compared to others in this book) you purposefully poured your life into your family and those in your circle. You made a difference in their lives, and they, in turn, are making a difference to the next generation, and the next. And so it goes.

A friend recently told me she wished she could do something that mattered, something with lasting value. I looked at her stirring a pot of homemade chicken-and-dumplings and held out my arm toward her children sweetly playing nearby. "You are!" I said. "When you pour yourself into them, you are!" Thank you, Mom Frey, for teaching me and countless others that in anonymity and the simple life of a homemaker we can find our high calling by loving our families with deeds, not just words.

Thank you for teaching me what you wrote at the end of your "List of Important Things": "Each of us, using our influence, can change the world around us, and like the waves of the ocean, have an impact on the whole world."

Sincerely,

Lindsey

One Last Thing

*W*hen we make the time to shift our focus from our own lives to that of another, good things happen. Getting lost, even momentarily, in someone else's story makes us think about our own, allows us to see from a different perspective, and lets us view God at work in the lives of others. Above all, we can learn from their stories, from both their triumphs and their failures. God has stirred my heart through looking into the lives of these women. I trust that your heart was stirred as well.

I noticed a few things that were common to these women as I read about them. Many were women of discipline, manifested in different ways. All of them were women of self-denial. Our natural human predisposition and our environment propels us to look for the easy road (after all, we "deserve a break today" and "we're worth it"), but many who made a difference were women willing to look beyond their own comforts, ease, fun, and fulfillment. They were dedicated to a greater cause: their children. And that is something all of us can do with God's strength.

Our children are too important for us not to grasp that shaping their lives is a blessing and high privilege. As Amy Carmichael says, "It is a solemn thing, however one regards it, to have to do with the moulding of a child—that wax which so quickly becomes marble, as someone has said. Nothing is unimportant in the trifles of nursery life, and nothing is so rewarding as the nurture of little children."

Not a single day of motherhood is ever wasted. Perhaps as you've read this book you've thought about your experiences with your own mother, questioned how you're doing as a mother, or wondered how your children will someday perceive the job you did in raising them. Those issues are settled for the moms in this book—the last chapter has already been written in their stories. We are still writing ours. When we sow seeds in the nurturing of our little ones, igniting within them a deep love for God, who knows, we just might change the world. But more importantly, we will be investing in the world to come.

Recommended Resources

Chapter One—Susanna Wesley

On a learning environment in the home:

- *For the Children's Sake*, Susan Schaeffer Macaulay (This is one of my favorite books. It's about awakening your child's mind and giving him or her a richer life.)
- *The Homeschool Journey: Windows into the Heart of a Learning Family*, Susan and Michael Card

On Discipline and the Home:

- *The 15 Minute Home and Family Organizer*, Emilie Barnes
- *The Stay-at-Home Mom*, Donna Otto
- *Disciplines of the Beautiful Woman*, Anne Ortlund
- *Celebration of Discipline,* Richard J. Foster

On the People:

- *Susanna Wesley*, Kathy McReynolds
- *John Wesley*, Basil Miller
- *The Man from Aldersgate: John Wesley*, video, Gospel Films

Chapter Two—Margaret Ruskin

On Imparting Scripture to Children:

- Awana Clubs International: One East Bode Rd., Streamwood, IL 60107
- *"GT and the Halo Express"* (Cassette tapes that teach Scripture to children through music. My kids love these.)
- *The Greenleaf Guide to Old Testament History*, Rob and Cyndy Shearer (Although not a Scripture memory program, this is a great first history

course—the history of Israel. Call 1-800-311-1508 for the Greenleaf
Press catalog.)

On Ruskin:

- *Praeterita*, John Ruskin (his autobiography)

Chapter Three—Monica

On Intercession:

- *When Mothers Pray*, Cheri Fuller
- *Praying the Bible for Your Children*, David and Heather Kopp
- *Becoming a Woman of Prayer*, Cynthia Heald
- *The Power of a Praying Parent*, Stormie Omartian

On Augustine:

- *Augustine of Hippo*, Peter Brown
- *Confessions*, St. Augustine (Look for the Pine-Coffin or Fulton Sheen translations.)

Chapter Four—Mary Bell Washington

On Instilling Character in our Children:

- *Your Child's Heart*, Terry Glaspey (An excellent book on nurturing moral values in our children.)
- *Worldproofing Your Kids*, Lael Arrington (The subtitle explains it well: Helping moms prepare their kids to navigate today's turbulent times. This book is Francis Schaeffer, with an Erma Bombeck twist.)
- *Raising a Modern-Day Knight*, Robert Lewis
- The Heritage Builders' *"Family Night Tool Chest"* series, Jim Weidmann and Kurt Bruner:

    —*Christian Character Qualities*
    —*Wisdom Life Skills*
    —*An Introduction to Family Nights*
    —*Basic Christian Beliefs*

On Washington:

- *George Washington the Christian*, William J. Johnstone (a 1919 publication reprinted and available from the God and Country Foundation [listed below] or the Mount Vernon Gift Shop at 703-780-2000.)
- *The Light and the Glory*, Peter Marshall & David Manuel
- *The Light and the Glory for Children*, Peter Marshall & David Manuel

- Mount Vernon's web site: www.mountvernon.org
- George Washington's Rules of Civility are available at: www.virginia.edu/gwpapers/civility/civ-tran.html
- God and Country Foundation, an organization dedicated to sharing the founding faith of America's Founding Fathers (one page flyers and books available): Box 75, Mount Vernon, VA, 22121, and their website: www.geocities.com/CapitolHill/Congress/1125
- Mary Ball Washington Museum and Library, RR 3 at Lancaster Court House, P.O. Box 97, Lancaster, VA, 804-462-7280.
- Mary Washington House, 1200 Charles St., Fredericksburg, VA 22401, 703-373-1569. (This was her final home purchased by George Washington in 1772, now an authentically furnished historic site.)
- Mary Washington Monument, 1500 Washington Ave., Fredericksburg, VA 22401, 703-373-3381. (This is the only U.S. monument erected to a woman by women. It marks the approximate site of her unmarked grave on the original Kenmore estate.)

Chapter Five—Jochebed

On Overcoming Fear:

- *Tame Your Fears*, Carol Kent

On Jochebed and Other Biblical Women:

- Exodus 1:15–2:10
- *All the Women of the Bible*, Edith Deen
- *Jochebed: Choosing to Trust* (A teaching tape with a wonderful dramatic interpretation by Jennie Dimkoff, 338 E. Main St., Fremont, MI 49412, $4.75.)

Chapter Six—Pioneer Moms

On Developing Personal Character:

- *Trusting God*, Jerry Bridges
- *Becoming a Woman of Excellence*, Cynthia Heald

On Pioneer Women:

- *Women of the West*, Cathy Lee Luchetti

Chapter Seven—Helena

On Serving Where You Are:

- *Woman of Influence: Ten Traits of Those Who Want to Make a Difference*, Pam Farrel

On Helena and Constantine:

- *The Emperor Constantine*, a play by Dorothy L. Sayers
- *Helena*, a novel by Evelyn Waugh

Chapter Eight—Catherine Carmichael

On Training Them Up as Individuals:

- *Bringing Out the Best in Your Child*, Cynthia Ulrich Tobias and Carol Funk (This book describes how what we see as our child's worst traits may be their best qualities.)

On Serving Others:

- *Improving Your Serve,* Charles Swindoll.
- *Watchman on the Walls*, Arkins & Harrell. (This book has a chapter on developing servanthood in your kids, as well as imparting other character qualities, through prayer.)

On Letting Them Go:

- *Give Them Wings*, Carol Kykendahl

On Amy Carmichael:

- *A Chance to Die: The Life and Legacy of Amy Carmichael*, Elisabeth Elliot
- *Amy Carmichael*, Kathleen White (sixth grade–high school)

By Amy Carmichael:

- 12 of her books available from Christian Literature Crusade, including *Gold Cord* and *God's Missionary*
- *Whispers of His Power* (Fleming H. Revell)
- *If* (Zondervan)

Chapter Nine—Mom Frey

On Leaving a Legacy Through Our Actions:

- *The Power of Mother Love*, Brenda Hunter, Ph.D. (About empowering us to mother from the heart. Beautiful.)
- *The Hidden Art of Homemaking*, Edith Schaeffer. (A classic.)
- *The Heritage*, J. Otis Ledbetter and Kurt Bruner.

Notes

Chapter 1: Susanna Wesley

1. Robert G. Tuttle, Jr., *John Wesley: His Life and Theology* (Grand Rapids, MI: Francis Asbury Press, 1978), 176.
2. Arnold A. Dallimore, *Susanna Wesley: The Mother of John & Charles Wesley* (Grand Rapids, MI: Baker Book House, 1993), 11.
3. Ibid., 57.
4. Sandy Dengler, *Susanna Wesley: Servant of God* (Chicago, IL: Moody Press, 1987), 162.
5. Dallimore, *Susanna Wesley: The Mother,* 57.
6. George J. Stevenson, *Memorials of the Wesley Family* (Partridge, 1876), 164, as quoted in Dallimore.
7. Dallimore, *Susanna Wesley: The Mother,* 61.
8. Ruth A. Tucker and Walter L. Liefeld, *Daughters of the Church* (Grand Rapids, MI: Zondervan, 1987), 237.
9. Ibid.
10. Dallimore, *Susanna Wesley: The Mother.* 90-91.
11. Stevenson, 281.
12. J.B. Wakeley, *Anecdotes of the Wesleys: Illustrative of Their Character and Personal History* (New York: Nelson & Phillips, 1869), found at http://gbgm-umc.org/UMW/Wesley/susanna1.html.
13. Tucker and Liefeld, *Daughters,* 238.
14. Dallimore, *Susanna Wesley: The Mother,* 157.

Chapter 2: Margaret Ruskin

1. John Ruskin, *Praeterita* (Boston: Dana Estes & Company Publishers, 1889), 35.
2. Ibid., 36.
3. Ibid., 35.
4. Van Akin Burd, ed., *The Ruskin Family Letters* (Ithaca: Cornell University Press, 1973), 145.
5. Ibid., 145.
6. Ibid.

Chapter 3: Monica

1. Richard Price, *Augustine*, "Great Christian Thinkers" series (Liguori, MO: Triumph, 1997), I.
2. J.D. Douglas, *Who's Who in Christian History* (Wheaton, IL: Tyndale House Publishers, 1992), 52.
3. Raymond Brown, *Giants of the Faith: Classic Christian Writings and the Men Behind Them* (Wheaton, IL: Crossway Books, 1997), 50.
4. Augustine, *Confessions* (New York: Penguin, 1961), 101.
5. Ibid., 178.
6. Ibid., 112.

Chapter Four: Mary Ball Washington

1. William Worthington Fowler, *Women on the American Frontier* (Detroit: Gale Research Company, 1974), 511.
2. Ibid., 509.
3. Frederick Bernays Wiener, "Washington and His Mother," *American History Illustrated*, July/August 1991, 68.
4. Marion Harland, *The Story of Mary Washington,* quoted in William Johnstone, *Washington the Christian* (Milford, MI: Mott Media, 1985), 39.
5. Ibid., 72.
6. William J. Johnstone, *George Washington the Christian* (Milford, MI: Mott Media, 1985), 19.
7. Ibid.
8. Fowler, *Women,* 511-12.
9. John N. Norton, *Life of General Washington*, 1870, 34.

Chapter Five: Jochebed

1. A.W. Pink, *Gleanings in Exodus* (Chicago: Moody Press, 1981), 16.
2. Edith Deen, *All the Women of the Bible* (New York: Harper Collins, 1955), 53.

Chapter Six: Pioneer Moms

1. William W. Fowler, *Women on the American Frontier* (Hartford: S.S. Scranton & Co., 1878), 22-23.
2. Harriet Sigerman, *Land of Many Hands: Women in the American West* (New York: Oxford University Press, 1997), 74.
3. Ibid., 73.
4. Cathy Lee Luchetti, *Women of the West* (St. George, Utah: Antelope Island Press, 1982), 64.
5. Peter Marshall and David Manuel, *From Sea to Shining Sea* (Grand Rapids: Fleming H. Revell, 1986), 344.
6. Fowler, *Women,* retold from the story on 250-60.
7. Ibid., 27-31.

8. *The Journal of Mollie Dorsie Sanford,* 2-3.
9. Ibid., 81.
10. Ibid., 32-33.
11. Ibid., 144.
12. Ibid.
13. Ibid., 137.
14. Ibid., 139.
15. Ibid., 176.
16. Ibid., 177.
17. Ibid., 178.
18. Ibid., 193.

Chapter 7: Helena

1. Taken from http://myron.sjsu.edu/romeweb/LADYCONT/art23.htm
2. Edith Deen, *Great Women of the Christian Faith* (Uhrichsville, OH: Barbour Publishing, Inc., 1986), 10.

Chapter 8: Catherine Carmichael

1. Elisabeth Elliot, *A Chance to Die: The Life and Legacy of Amy Carmichael* (Grand Rapids, MI: Fleming H. Revell, 1987), 26.
2. Kathleen White, *Amy Carmichael* (Minneapolis: Bethany House, 1986), 12.
3. Elliot, *A Chance,* 26.
4. White, *Amy,* 7.
5. Elizabeth Skoglund, *Amma: The Life and Words of Amy Carmichael* (Grand Rapids, MI: Baker Books, 1994), 17.
6. White, *Amy,* 11.
7. Elliot, *A Chance,* 30.
8. Ibid., 55.
9. Sources for this section taken from Elliot, *A Chance,* 52-56 and White, *Amy,* 36-39.

If you would like to contact the author, write to:

Lindsey O'Connor
PO Box 1716
Castle Rock, CO 80104